D0364573

for

BOYS

only

FRANK HOWARD RICHARDSON, M.D.

for BOYS only

The Doctor Discusses the Mysteries of Manhood

DAVID McKAY COMPANY, INC.

Nineteenth Printing, April, 1970

Manufactured in the United States of America

FOREWORD

By HIGHT C. MOORE, D.D.
Editorial Secretary of Sunday School Board, Southern Baptist Convention. Recording Secretary of Southern Baptist Convention (retired)

FOR BOYS ONLY IS FOR BOYS FIRST AND MAINLY. WHILE not primarily for parents and teachers, scoutmasters and child specialists, these will find it serviceable to read, and recommend, and place in their home, school and church libraries.

Knowing boys better than they know themselves, Dr. Richardson is a magnetic personality in their midst. He is past master of their phraseology; posted as to their peculiarities and preferences; director of their pastimes in camp or on campus; inspirer of the best in them; and guide in their efforts to prepare themselves for maximum efficiency.

In all his talks, and especially in the secrets of sex, he is revealing without repelling; strict but not stern; sympathetic while restraining wrong desires; never coercive though firmly corrective; and always cooperative, constructive and conscientious.

Our genial author is accessible to any boy who is aspiring, inquiring or even inquisitive. They call him "Doc" and tell him everything quite frankly. He has the exact angle of approach, appeal and personal application. Whether in his private office, in their classrooms, or on their campgrounds, he meets them with engaging cordiality, chats with apparent (though carefully planned) informality, and welcomes their questions that bristle and sparkle.

Thus the bright boy is instructed, aroused and stimulated. And the dull boy is encouraged to realize that he is not nearly so dull as he thinks himself, as he sharpens his wits on the whetstone provided for him. Thus each is helped to become a bigger, braver and better boy.

In this volume are crystallized the author's activities and attainments in varied localities and diverse fields. He was a gifted lad with versatile experiences in city and country, seaside and mountains, North and South. He is a good father of three sons and two daughters, whose success in their chosen lines gladdens his heart while it testifies to his personal and professional ability. He is a beloved physician in our Southern Highlands, an expert and popular specialist in the care and cure of children, and withal a writer of rare ability and wide acceptance, as certified by his books and articles in many magazines.

"If you've read this book through," as the author tells us in his last chapter, "you've learned something about how boys and men are made." You've realized, too, that "growing up completely means, sooner or later, getting married and having boys and perhaps girls of your own." And you've come to appreciate that "growing up isn't something anyone can do, like rolling off a log,—it takes effort, and plenty of it."

HIGHT C. MOORE

CONTENTS

CONTENTS

INTRODUCTION

By Wilburt C. Davison, M.A., D.Sc., LL.D., M.D.
Department of Pediatrics, Duke University School of Medicine

THE MOST DIFFICULT PERIOD OF A BOY'S LIFE IS THAT between elementary school and high school. While in elementary school he is told what to do and why; and by the time he becomes a high school senior he usually knows what he wants to do and why. But in that interval of adolescence during early high school while he is becoming an adult, he is bewildered not only by the physical changes he is undergoing but by the emotional behavior caused by these physical changes.

Dr. Richardson's book supplies in a most interesting way the information he wants and needs. After a boy has read this book he knows why he does the things which often lead to trouble, why he tries to outdrive other motorists, why he imitates the love life of older men, and why he must attempt to convince himself and others that he is bigger, smarter and more courageous than he really knows himself to be.

Dr. Richardson doesn't preach; but he answers the questions which bubble through every boy's mind at this period, questions on sex and other problems which he often hesitates to ask, for usually there is no one to whom he can unburden himself without embarrassment and from whom he can obtain straight facts.

This book will fill an urgent need for the adolescent youth. But it will be of inestimable help as well to family doctors and pediatricians. For these men are becoming increasingly conscious that advice to youngsters of this group is not only necessary but also will go far toward reducing the behavior problems which are so frequent in this generation.

for BOYS only

IT'S A WRECK

THE SIREN WAILED AT A HIGH PITCH. AND DOWN THE pike raced the wrecker closely followed by an ambulance. They stopped, with shrieking brakes, just as Jack and the doctor reached the scene of the accident. The crowd, already milling round two jammed hulks that a few minutes before had been shiny new sedans, stood aside to open up a passage for the doctor's car. As he stopped he saw two highway patrolmen dragging the apparently lifeless form of a fifteen-year-old boy from the driver's seat of one of the cars.

Jack, who does odd jobs for the doctor, was finishing his daily chore of sweeping the office sidewalk when a phone call had summoned the doctor to an accident a half mile out of town. Snatching up his emergency bag and calling "Hop in, Jack, if you want to come along," the doctor had jumped into his coupé, stepped on the starter, jammed the accelerator down to the floor, and they were off, swinging into the highway just behind the ambulance. Now, leaving the car, he pushed his way through the crowd that clustered round the unconscious form of the young driver, then asked everyone to stand back so as to give the boy some air.

After a brief but thorough going over, during which he

examined the lad's eye reflexes, and moved his arms, legs and body very gently to make sure there were no broken bones, the doctor rose to his feet. "He has a slight concussion, but probably no brain injury, luckily for him. Get him into the ambulance, and take him home and put him to bed. I'll come by and see him again in a few minutes, just as soon as I'm through here," and he turned to look over any other occupants of the wrecked cars that might need his help.

§

"Harry's a lucky boy," said the doctor next morning, as he finished his examination and pronounced the lad O.K. He had found him sitting up and feeling fine, apparently none the worse for his adventure of the day before.

"Oh, good morning, Mr. Taylor," he nodded to Harry's father who had entered the room as he was leaving. "How that son of yours escaped from that head-on crash with nothing more serious than a temporary concussion and a few scratches is more than I can understand or explain. He's a very lucky lad, indeed."

Mr. Taylor interrupted angrily: "Lucky? *I* don't see anything lucky about it. That's the second brand new car he's wrecked, and he has had a half dozen very close squeaks. And invariably it's been because of some road hog who had no right to try to pass him. Each time he's tried to show them they couldn't get ahead of *him*. You can see what he *has* showed them—and showed me, too! I call it the worst kind of luck—though I can't blame him for being angry, and trying to teach them a lesson." The baffled father grunted something under his breath that sounded very much like an oath, uncertain which to blame most—his reckless son, or the irresponsible motorists who had tempted the boy to take these ill-fated chances. Meanwhile Harry, who up till then had been chatting pleasantly enough with the doctor, gave his father a look as black as a thundercloud. Noticing it, the doctor turned toward the bed.

"Your dad and I are both wrong, Harry—I for saying you were lucky, and he for blaming your bad luck for your troubles. It's not your bad luck that makes you wreck your dad's cars—it's losing your temper like a dumb adolescent, instead of acting like a man and letting other drivers kill themselves instead of ruining you.

"Mr. Taylor, if you'll forgive me for offering some advice you haven't asked me for, it's partly your fault for agreeing with Harry when he tries to spite these other drivers. Instead of explaining to him by quiet reasoning how foolish it is to try to assert his rights, you just scold him a bit and then let him go ahead and wreck another car. If he can't control *himself*, he's not old enough to try to drive a car that he can't control."

By this time Mr. Taylor looked pretty much like a thundercloud, too; but then he broke in with a short laugh:

"You're his doctor. If it's just adolescence that's ailing him, why don't you teach him how to manage it and control himself?"

"I'll do better than that. We're going to have a discussion down at school this week and we'll talk about driving cars and getting along with fathers too, before we get through. I'll be looking for you, Harry," and the door closed behind him.

I'LL BE THERE

IT WAS JUST A FEW MINUTES BEFORE TIME FOR THE school football game to begin when Jack knocked at the doctor's door, then came in rather bashfully. "Mother wants me to get something from you to cure these pimples that have been bothering me. I don't see why it is that so many of the fellows in my class have this messy skin trouble. Some of them aren't so bad; but others are much worse than I am, with big red bumps and boils that have to be lanced. What causes it, anyway, doctor?"

"That's quite a long story, Jack. I'm sure you'd be interested in it, and I'd love to talk to you about it. It opens up something I'm quite sure every boy wants to know about. Strangely enough, it has to do with the very thing I was talking to your friend Harry about yesterday. I wish we had time to talk about it now, but we haven't. But I'm going . . ."

"Yeah, I saw Harry today, and he tells me that Prof has asked you to come to school and talk to us about some of the things that puzzle us, and that we can't find answers to. Prof says you do this every year. I'd sure like to hear what goes on there."

"That's right. I talk to the fellows for a while; and then

they pop any questions at me they want to, and I try my best to answer them. Some of them are really humdingers with no holds barred. But right now you are on your way to the game, and I've got some calls to make.

"Save up your questions and tell any of the fellows you see to do the same. We always have a big time at these parties. After the general questions are over and chapel is dismissed, anyone is free to come down to the front and ask me anything he wants to, about any personal matter he might not like to have talked about in front of the whole school."

"Gee, that sounds great," said Jack. "I sure want to be there. And I'll bet you *will* get some humdingers, from what I've heard some of the fellows say when no one's around," and he grinned in anticipation of seeing the doctor squirm.

"So long, then, Jack. I'll be seeing you." And the doctor turned back into the house. As Jack hurried along the street, he was already wondering what questions he'd be hearing, and what he himself might ask, when the doctor came to school within the next few days.

FROM BOY TO MAN

ONE DAY, THE FOLLOWING WEEK, THE DOCTOR APPEARED on the chapel platform and began his talk:

Prof has asked me to come here this morning and talk with you about some of the things fellows talk about when older people are not around, because they know folks aren't supposed to discuss such matters. But, as you can imagine, a doctor gets all kinds of questions thrown at him. He has so many different sorts that he gets used to being surprised, and nothing fazes him. It's my business to try to help people, not to judge them or criticize them.

This morning, after I've told you some of the things I know all of you have been wondering and talking about, I'm going to let you ask me anything you want to. We won't have any kid stuff, like giggling and snickering when some fellow asks something you don't usually hear talked about out in the open. Let's really find out some things we'd like to know about this morning.

Now some of you may think you know just the person who can tell you everything along this line you need to know. You think it's the big guy in the class ahead of you who's "been around" and is quite sure he knows all the answers. He may like to sound off and show you how wise he is, but don't let him fool you. He doesn't know much more about these things than you do. What's worse, a lot of what he knows just isn't so!

So give him a brush-off when he tries to impress you with how much he knows, and how innocent and green you are. It will be much better to rely on someone who really knows, and can give you straight answers.

I'm going to try to be that person this morning, or any other time you may care to come to me and ask me something. If you stump me with something, I'll find somebody who knows the answer, and send you to him, or bring his answer back to you.

So now, let's go.

Probably every fellow here this morning has wondered why it is that somewhere around the age that you are now, certain changes begin to take place in your body that are different from anything you've ever known before. Your voice begins to go haywire every once in a while when you are singing, and even at specially important and sometimes very embarrassing times when you're talking.

Then, too, your skin may start showing blackheads—those ugly little black dots that come out when you squeeze them, followed by a little white waxy stuff. Keeping your face clean doesn't prevent them coming, either. Squeezing blackheads sometimes causes infection, and they turn first into red bumps and then into painful boils. Your skin, that you never used to notice, may feel greasy or dry and scaly and uncomfortable; you think everybody is noticing how bad it makes you look.

Another of these changes is the gradual appearance of hair on different parts of your body—under your armpits, in your groins, and on your cheeks and upper lip. No, you haven't got a mustache yet, but it looks as if you might be starting one. Some of you have even taken a crack at Dad's razor or electric shaver. (Better put it back exactly where he keeps it, if you have. He's probably touchy about such things).

Possibly what's bothered you more than anything else, is that you've begun to be clumsy as you never used to be when you were smaller and younger. You sometimes stumble over your big feet when you come into a room, especially if there happen to be strangers there and you feel a little bit uncomfortable in front of them. Maybe you knock over a glass of water at the table when you reach for it with those long arms of yours, which is pretty unpleasant if the folks are having company. You never used to be so clumsy and do such awkward things. Why should you suddenly get that way, now that you are older and ought to have *more* control instead of *less?* "What's the matter with me, anyway?" you think.

But there certainly can't be any connection between all of these entirely different things, you'd naturally think. Well, if you think that, you are wrong, all wrong. They are all parts of a very strange change that everybody goes through when about the age you fellows are now. They're part of a kind of growth that's entirely different from any growth you've ever gone through, or even known about, before.

Up to now, you've been growing gradually and steadily, first from small to big, and next from big to bigger, with no change except one of size, as an animal or a tree grows. But now a growth or change has come along that is something of a different kind entirely. For it is a complete alteration that is taking place, that marks you as being no longer a boy, but a beginning man—though it may take years yet before the change is completed. And the thing that brings all this about is what you've learned in your biology class to call the "glandular system."

You know of course about the glands that manufacture fluids for doing things in the body that we know about, like the gastric (stomach) and intestinal glands that pour out digestive juices; the skin glands that furnish sweat and oil to keep the skin in good condition; and the tear glands that gave us something to cry with when we were children. We call these glands of external secretion.

But there are other glands that manufacture something that goes into our bodies and works in a way harder to understand. One of these, the pituitary gland, is a little thing tucked away under the brain that makes our bodies grow big enough, but not too big. Another is the thyroid gland, that makes us alert and keeps us on our toes. If it becomes too active, we get terribly nervous and scary and jittery and big-eyed. But if it's not active enough, we get sluggish and stupid and dull. We call these glands of internal secretion; because while we can see the results they cause, we can't see what they produce as we can in the case of the glands of external secretion I've just mentioned.

There's still a third kind of gland which turns out *both* external *and* internal secretions. One of these, or rather two of these, are the testicles, two plum-sized glands that are contained in a bag called the scrotum, that hangs down from the crotch, just back of the penis. We're going to call things by their real names here, you understand; for you lads are big enough now to discuss things like men, and not like kids that have to have baby names for parts of your body, or the functions that they perform.

The internal secretion put out by the testicles is the peculiar fluid that starts off all these changes of growth that you've been noticing in yourselves—the overactivity of the skin glands, the voice changes, the appearance of hair in different parts of the body, and the sudden spurt in height and weight that makes you stumble over your clodhopper feet, and fumble things when you miss your aim with your long arms. Stranger still, it brings about differences in the way you think and feel, that we call your emotional development.

This internal secretion put out by the testicles changes you in some mysterious way that no one really understands, so that you begin to feel the way a man feels and have some of the thoughts and wishes that a man has and that a younger boy doesn't have. For example, you begin to have courage and backbone and guts, that are not expected of a small boy but *are* taken for granted in a man. You get more and more interested in girls, where before as a little fellow you thought they were just a nuisance to be teased and then pushed aside. You look forward to having more to do with them—first with any girl, later with one particular one.

After a while you'll find you'd like to be with that girl for most of the time, if she turns out to be just the one you've been looking for. And at last you'll want to marry her and have her for your very own, and have children that are yours and hers. It will take some years before all this happens, of course; but that's what this mystery juice I'm talking about is already starting to do to you. So you see why I say it's so important.

Now don't fall for the idea that so many people have, that a deep rumbling voice, or lots of hair on chest and armpits and arms and legs, means that a person is more of a he-man than if these were not so pronounced. Many a star athlete has very little hair anywhere except what he wears on top of his head, and a voice that is absolutely tenor.

Every one passes through this stage of development that is called adolescence—from two word roots that mean "becoming adult"—unless for some reason, such as injury or disease, his testicles are unable to do their work. That is why it is so necessary for a boy to follow a doctor's directions after a severe blow is suffered by the testicle, or when he has mumps. Such care usually prevents any permanent damage that might otherwise take place.

The intentional prevention of the change called adolescence is what takes place when a bull is castrated and thereby changed into a mild-dispositioned ox. The same thing happens when a young stallion is turned into a steady-going horse, or a scrappy cocky rooster turns into a fat sluggish capon. In the middle ages this was sometimes done on boys with good singing voices, so that they wouldn't change from soprano or alto to tenor or bass. Such persons (called "eunuchs") became fat and flabby and sallow, with wide hips like a woman's. Fortunately, this is never done nowadays; so it need give us no concern here and now.

So much for the *internal* secretion of the testicles.

But what about the "external secretion" that I told you is manufactured by the testicles? This is extremely different, in its purpose and actions. It consists of millions of tiny bodies floating in a white substance, which is called "semen," or "spermatic fluid," because it contains the male elements that are called "sperms." One of these will some day leave the body to unite with a female element, the egg or "ovum," that is produced in the ovary of a girl or woman, and will form an "embryo," as the very beginning human being is called.

Each sperm or male element consist of a tiny head, and a wriggling tail about six times as long, that altogether measures not over one five hundredth of an inch in length! It is hard to believe that the union of two such tiny cells—(for the ovum isn't much larger) so small that they cannot be seen except under a high powered microscope, could ever grow into a seven- or eight-pound baby, or later into a man or woman of 150 or 160 pounds!

How do these sperms leave the body? There are several ways, that I'll tell you about later. But telling you this much has taken so long that I'll have to wait till another get-together before going into that. Right now, I'm ready for your questions. Send them along, and let's get started at once, so we'll have plenty of time for everyone. Who'll be the first to ask about something you've been wondering about?

QUESTIONS

AT THE END OF THE TALK, THE BOYS CAME DOWN TO THE front of the chapel and crowded around the doctor. The questions came quick and fast; and in order to make the most of what time was left, they had to be answered quickly and to the point. Here they are:

Question. Is it a sign that something is wrong when one testicle hangs down lower than the other?

Answer. No, that's the way it is with everyone. It's usually the left one that hangs lower, though sometimes it's the right. You've probably noticed that both hang down lower after a hot bath, while the scrotum gets tighter and less relaxed after a cold plunge or shower.

Question. What does it mean when there's a hard lump in the scrotum?

Answer. This is usually what is called a hydrocele, and is an accumulation of water. It may have to be drawn off by a surgeon through a hollow needle—not a serious operation at all. If there is a painful lump, however, that is probably an inflammation of the testicle, called orchitis. It should be treated at once, as it may be serious if it is neglected. For anything like this, go to your doctor at once.

Question. But if there's a soft irregular lump, that sometimes feels heavy and dragging down, especially after I've been standing or running or doing any heavy exercise; what is that from?

Answer. That is known as a varicocele. It is due to a weakening of the walls of the vein that carries the blood back from the testicle into the body. It's been described as feeling to the examining surgeon like a bunch of angle worms! It can be cured by a simple operation that consists in tying off the weakened vein so that the blood will flow back through other and stronger veins. But it is rarely uncomfortable enough to need any treatment at all.

Question. Is a rupture an indication that a boy isn't perfectly manly?

Answer. Not at all. It simply means that one part of the wall of muscle that keeps the intestine inside the abdomen has a weak spot that has allowed a knuckle or loop of intestine to protrude. Sometimes it can be held back in place by wearing a truss or support that exerts pressure on it, and thus reinforces the weak spot in the muscle wall. It's usually better to have a surgeon sew the sheathes of the muscles together in such a way that this spot is strengthened. It's not a serious operation. Some of the huskiest athletes develop hernias after strenuous athletic exertion, and have to be operated on. So you see that a rupture, or hernia, is not a sign that a fellow is a weakling.

Question. Does it mean that a boy can never have children if he has only one testicle?

Answer. Not at all. It simply means that there has been a delay in the movement of one of these glands from inside the abdomen, where they are normally before birth, down into the scrotum. If it cannot be brought down by medicine or injections, a simple operation will do the trick.

Question. It is serious if a boy's nipples grow hard and swollen and tender?

Answer. That is a perfectly natural thing to take place during this time of developing into manhood that we've been talking about.

Question. Some of the bigger fellows sometimes pinch or twist a smaller boy's nipples through his clothes so that it hurts. Isn't there any danger in this?

Answer. Of course there is. Serious damage can occur as a result. Bullying a smaller lad is pretty small potatoes, especially when it can do as much harm as this silly custom does.

Question. What is it when the penis gets hard?—I mean, just what happens?

Answer. Some parts of the penis are spongy, containing very many tiny spaces, through which the blood circulates. Sometimes when a fellow gets to thinking about sex, or even when he is asleep, the return of blood gets cut off, and the organ becomes hard, larger, and rigid, like the fire engine hose under high pressure. When the mechanism for shutting off the returning blood relaxes, it returns to its usual limp, soft condition. This is called an erection.

Question. Some fellows are very sensitive because of the small size of these parts, especially younger boys. I've seen something advertised that is guaranteed to develop them and increase their size. Is there any need for such a thing, for fellows like this?

Answer. No, nor for anyone else. The size of the organs of generation has absolutely nothing to do with a person's manliness, or "virility," as it is called. Ads of this sort play on the false idea, based on ignorance, that large parts mean great sex ability. Nothing could be farther from the truth.

These advertisements are nothing but gold bricks, meant to wheedle money out of innocent boobs. They can't accomplish what they promise, of course; and even if they could, it would do no good.

Question. Do they develop faster in some people than in others?

Answer. Yes, just as some boys are slower in developing hair on their chests, and some people get teeth later than other people. For that matter, they never get as large in some men as they do in others; but this doesn't affect their sex life at all.

Question. Doesn't a shot of liquor increase a fellow's ability to be—er,—manly?

Answer. Not in the slightest. What it does do is simply to make him *think* he's more of a man than he actually is! Even a little drink makes a fellow's opinion of himself go up, while it strengthens his desires. At the same time it blunts the good sense and self-restraint that might otherwise have kept him from doing harm to a girl he's supposed to be reliable enough to be with. And its avoidance might well prevent him from getting a disease, or from becoming the father of an illegitimate child. You can imagine what a tragedy either of these must be!

That's all for today. See you again before too long.

TWO BIG PROBLEMS

"THERE, THAT TOUGH JOB IS OVER AND DONE WITH," growled the doctor, as the last of the group of prospective campers stepped off the office scale and started to dress. "You're none of you such perfect specimens of manhood, but at least every one of you has passed his physical exam for camp. Now hurry up and dress and get out of here so that I can get some worthwhile work done."

He started to leave the room, when he was halted by a chorus of howls and jeers. He turned round in time to see a flustered Tom stoop down and reclaim a bulldog briar pipe that had clattered to the floor from the pocket of the trousers some thoughtful friend had tied in a hard knot while he was on the scale.

"So what?" countered Tom belligerently. "You've all seen me smoke, even if Doc hasn't. As far as that goes, most of you do, too, though you're not men enough to come out and do it in the open.

"But when you come right down to it, what harm does it do us? Most of our dads and half our mothers smoke, and it hasn't killed them. Why should we wait till we're eighteen, or twenty one, or whatever it is they tell us to wait till, before we start? Go right ahead and say what you're thinking, though I know you don't approve, Doc."

It was a question they had all asked themselves. They looked expectantly at the doctor, knowing that he would give them the straight of it if they asked for it.

"Sit down and I'll tell you exactly what I think. You've used up half my lunch period, so I may as well waste another few minutes. How do you know I don't approve, Wise Guy? Did I ever let on that I knew that you, or any of the rest of you, were smoking? How do you suppose I could tell?" He caught Jim's hand and held it up so that everyone could see the yellow stains on his index and middle fingers. "Don't ask me why I'm such a keen private eye. It's perfectly simple," and the doctor smiled his exasperating smile.

"Of course you couldn't approve openly, or our folks would all say you were a 'bad influence,' " Tom defended himself. "But honestly, just what *is* wrong with smoking, anyway? I know you're not a smoker, yourself. Suppose you tell us why not, if you can take the time?" The boys squatted in a circle on the examining room floor, the doctor swung one leg over the examining table in what looked like an extremely uncomfortable position, but which he seemed to like, and began.

"In the first place, I don't consider it any of my business whether you smoke or not. I do think it's *your* business, though, to decide whether you're doing the square thing when you smoke behind your parents' backs. I've known lots of men, and a lot of doctors among them, who are convinced that there's no harm in their smoking. But I've never yet known anyone, even if he himself smoked behind the barn when he was ten, who would come out and say he believed smoking is desirable, or even that it's harmless, for a boy of fourteen or fifteen."

"But doesn't it stunt your growth? That's what my granddad says he always used to be told. But he's a pretty tough old six-footer; so it didn't seem to interfere with *his* growth," and Jack sat back with a satisfied smile, as if he had spiked at least one argument.

"It's extremely difficult for scientific observers to deliver an impartial verdict on such a very personal question as smoking," the doctor answered thoughtfully. "Doctors are much like other people—they do pretty much what they want to do, and then look around and try to find or make up reasons to justify themselves.

"I can refer you to what the writers honestly intend to be scientific articles, both for and against; but I can honestly say I don't know which are the more truly impartial and to be believed. Some doctors say smoking is bad for some forms of heart disease; others say that's nonsense, and that moderate smoking is calming to the nerves. Some observers are convinced that the undoubted increase in the number of cases of cancer of the lung has a definite relationship to the increase in smoking and especially inhaling of cigarette smoke. I certainly shouldn't dare to venture an opinion, when the authorities disagree."

"But *you* don't smoke; so you must think it's bad," suggested Jim.

"As for myself, I've never seen enough advantages in it to make me feel it was worth my while to begin. For I know that if I once did, I'd probably never quit. I know a lot of men and women that do try to stop, every once in a while, and they are miserable when they're not smoking. It's funny, but you never hear anybody rave over how much he enjoys it, while he *is* smoking.

"Some people have to be always doing something with

their hands; but I'm not the fidgety kind. Some folks, women especially, but a lot of men and boys, too, are 'slaves to fashion.' They just *have* to be doing what they think the majority of people are doing, or they feel out of line, and sort of inferior, or ill at ease. I've never felt that anyone cared a hoot whether I smoked or not. Most smokers never count up what the habit costs them. But you know, and I know, that it must cost plenty. I have a lot of ways to spend money that I get more fun out of. All in all, I can't see that the good things outweigh the disadvantages, for me—and for a lot of other folks as well. But that's *their* business, not mine.

"So now you know what I think about my smoking, and about yours. But don't think I'm going to snitch about Tom's pipe—or about Harry's coffin nails, either," and he deftly twitched a pack of a well-known brand from the shirt pocket of the boy who squatted at his feet. "Now hustle, or you'll be late to the basketball game," and he shooed the group into the hall.

As the boys trooped out, Harry called to Bill, "Hurry up, Romeo! Don't keep Anne waiting, or she'll be sitting the game out with your rival. Or maybe you'd rather go moping down Lover's Lane, or necking in the movies." Harry ducked Bill's swinging left, and the others grinned appreciatively, while Jack, the youngest, looked rather disgusted at the whole by-play.

Dropping behind as the others crowded out the door, Jack turned to the doctor with a puzzled air. The doctor waited encouragingly, and the boy began:

"I say, doctor, just what *is* the fun in what the older fellows are always beating their gums about—petting, or necking, or boodling? Is it the same as what the older people used to call spooning? How can a fellow who's as good an athlete and all-round outdoor man as Bill, stand it to stay hanging around with some girl who isn't interested in a single thing a boy enjoys doing? I just don't get it."

"You will before too long, Jack; you will. Do you remember what I told you fellows in school the other day about the changes that take place in your bodies about the age you are now? Well, there are other changes that you're probably just beginning to notice, though as yet you're just a little ashamed to admit it.

"Up until a little while ago, you weren't the least bit interested in girls, and you couldn't understand why the other fellows were such saps as to fall for them, and the sissy stuff that went with it all.

"But now you're beginning to have a change in the way you feel about them, though it makes you mad to have to admit it. Before, all the use you had for girls was to tease them, and be mean to them, and feel how superior you were to them. Now you don't know why it is, but you kinda like to be with them—or maybe to be with one particular certain one of them. The other fellows are beginning to notice it, and they rag you about it. You get back by riding some other boy for doing and feeling the same way you do.

"So far, you just like to be with her and talk with her; though you're ashamed to have anybody notice it. But a little while later on, when more of that change from boy to man that we talked about gets to working in you, you'll want to get close to her, and put your arm around her, and maybe even kiss her. Or maybe it'll be some other girl you feel that way about. It would be very unusual if this change didn't take place in you.

"Now a certain amount of this is, as I say, perfectly all right. But after a while it is likely to go too far, and get to the point of wanting to be closer and closer, so that you may suddenly wake up and find that you feel terribly like doing something you know you ought not to do, like touching other parts of her body.

"Some day, when you are a little bit farther along on this road that every boy has to travel, I'll talk with you some more about it. But that's as far as we need to go today, anyway. If you'll only remember to do what you know is right, you can have a whale of a good time with girls. And what's more, you'll be doing the square thing by them and by yourself. Meanwhile, don't be too scornful about the way Bill and some of the other older Joes are acting. You'll be there yourself the first thing you know.

"Now get going and catch up with the rest of the mob. Get into the cheering section and yell your head off for your team. If one particular girl is where she can see you, I'll bet you'll split a lung trying to outdo the others—but you won't admit it. G'bye now," and the door closed behind the doctor, as Jack walked slowly down the street, uncertain as to how much of what had been said was really true.

GIRLS

TWO WEEKS LATER THE DOCTOR AGAIN FOUND HIMSELF on the chapel platform before a hundred eager listeners waiting for him to take up where he had left off. He began with no introduction:

When I saw you before, I told you that the next time we discussed things I was going to explain to you how the sperms, or male cells, left a boy's body, and what happened to them. But after thinking it over I have decided that something else ought to come first. I shall, therefore, describe to you how a girl's or woman's body differs from ours, and tell you something of its function in this business of making more people so as to keep up the supply of folks in this world of ours.

Now I know that many of you fellows have been told all sorts of things that aren't so—sometimes by people that don't know any better, and sometimes by folks that are just plain lying. Nobody likes being played for a sucker; so I am going to give you the straight of it. If I don't make things clear, interrupt and stop me as we go along; or ask anything you want to after I've finished.

You remember, don't you, that I told you last time about

the three different kinds of glands—external secretion, internal secretion, and both kinds at once—and that the testicles belong to the third class, those that have both external and internal secretions. If you have given it any thought at all, you've probably guessed that girls and women must have some glands that are somewhat like these, that perform the same duties. For in the first place there would have to be some sort of female cells to unite with the male cells to make new people. And in the second place, there would have to be something to change little girls into big girls, and then into women, as they grow older, just as you and I have to be changed from boys into men.

If you reasoned this way, you'd be what they call a "logician"—a fellow who uses his head to reason out the causes that bring about certain effects. And you'd be dead right. For there *are* such glands; and they are very much like the testicles in a man or boy. They do produce another magic fluid that can't be seen, but that changes girls and makes them grow up into women, who act so different and look so different from the way we boys and men do. And at the same time, they manufacture female cells that can join with male cells to make the beginnings of new human beings. These glands are called the ovaries.

If you've ever had a bad stomach ache, bad enough to call the doctor for, you'll probably remember how he poked around all over your poor sore tummy, but especially on the lower right side, to see whether you had appendicitis. Well, near this spot in girls lies the right ovary; and in the same spot on the left side, the left ovary. They are about the same size and shape as the testicles; and they act in girls just about the same way that the testicles do in boys. They never get outside of the body, though, the way the testicles do, but always stay inside the abdomen, just as the testicles did before birth.

They produce an internal secretion that causes girls to change into women. About every four weeks they produce an egg (ovum, in Latin). Let's see what happens to this ovum—where it goes, and what organ in the body receives it, and what becomes of it.

Lying right between the two ovaries there's a hollow organ about the size and shape of a small pear, called the womb, or uterus. A tiny tube runs from this to each ovary; and along one of these tubes a tiny egg travels from the ovary to the uterus each month. Each is about 1/125 of an inch across. That is quite a little larger than the sperms I told you about last time.

If a male cell meets this egg somewhere in its course along the tube from the ovary to the uterus and unites with it, we say that it has become fertilized; and an embryo is what is formed. That's the way life began for every one of us here, and for every other human being that ever was born. Pretty big jump from a speck so small you can't see it without a microscope, to a big lug like one of you, wasn't it? Then this tiny fertilized seed has to travel to the uterus, where it will be allowed to grow for the next nine months.

Now what do you suppose the womb does so that it can take care of such an egg, if it gets fertilized? For it has to get ready for that job every month, even if it never receives a fertilized egg. It does this by thickening its lining so as to provide a warm cozy nest where the fertilized egg, or embryo, can be fed and kept warm for nine months until it is ready to leave the uterus and come out into the world as a live baby.

But if it doesn't get fertilized—and of course it is only very rarely that it does—then it has to be thrown out of the body.

And along with it at the same time go shreds of this thickened lining, together with a certain amount of blood. But this doesn't happen in a minute or a few minutes—it may take as long as a week, or as little time as three days. As it happens every month, more or less, it is called the monthly flow, or menstrual period (from the Latin word for month).

While this is perfectly normal, it is a time of discomfort for some girls; and they are advised not to do any very hard exercise nor to bathe in very cold water at these times. So if a girl tells you that she can't go on a hike or play some active game or go swimming when she's made a date to do so, it's good sense to know there's probably a sound reason. Don't be dumb and ask too many questions.

That reminds me that it doesn't hurt any boy to remember once in a while that no matter how much of a tomboy a girl may be, she can't be expected to be quite so rugged and tough as a boy. Instead of teasing her and trying to make her feel inferior, a fellow shows himself a much better sport if he gives her a break and a helping hand once in a while. It's the guy that's really tough and rugged and strong that doesn't have to keep throwing his weight around to show people how good he is.

Now come on down here in front, any of you who want to stick me with questions. I'll do my best to answer 'em as fast as you can put 'em across.

MORE QUESTIONS

THE BOYS WERE A LITTLE SLOW ABOUT OPENING UP ON this rather unfamiliar topic. But they thawed quickly and showed interest when one of the younger teachers, a fellow quite popular with the boys, and especially with the football squad, stepped up and asked:

Question. Haven't you seen ads in drug stores and magazines telling girls they don't have to take care during their periods, but can dance and swim and hike just the same as at other times? Yet you seem to tell us just the opposite. Which is right—you, or the ads?

Answer. Both of us. You'll remember I said *some* girls have considerable discomfort; that they shouldn't indulge in *hard* exercise, or bathe in *very cold* water. The ads are talking about girls *in general;* but a boy doesn't know whether the girl in question is, or is not, one of these. So I say it's better to play safe and not be either nosey or persistent if a girl seems to want to skip a date.

Question. Why is it, if as you say it's so terrible for a girl to let a boy go too far, that so many of them try to lead a fellow along and tease him into trying to do what you say he ought not to do?

Answer. That's a question with a whole lot of possible answers. Some girls are unhappy at home, and would be glad to spite their parents by doing things they know they would feel bad to have their daughter do. Some like to show their power over boys, and brag of their "conquests" to the other girls. And some girls don't realize how much easier it is for a boy to get excited than it is for them; and how much harder it is for a boy to stop, once he's started, though sometimes it's the other way round.

Question. Is that why so many girls dress so as to show off the shape of their breasts, or other parts of their body that boys would think they ought to keep covered, if they were girls of the right sort—and yet we know that a lot of those who do this are really the nicest sort of girls?

Answer. That's another tricky question that it would take us much too long to try to answer completely here. Some do it because they think it's the smart thing to imitate the movie stars. More do it, I imagine, because it's the fashion; and some folks would pass out if they didn't follow the fashions. Some do it, as I said just now, to tease boys along and see what they'll do. And many others don't stop to think what effect it may have on the boys that take them out, when they go to places where it's easy to forget what's right and what's wrong. And there are still other girls who are honestly and truly too innocent, or too ignorant, to know how such things impress fellows, and what they naturally think about the morals of the girls who dress that way. Even their mothers may not know how boys think and feel about such things; while many fathers have forgotten about how they felt when they were boys.

Question. Is there any harm in kissing a girl goodnight, or holding hands in the dark in the moving pictures, especially when they're having pretty warm close-ups?

Answer. Well, I'd say that depends pretty much on how you feel about the girl you're with when you're doing it. If it makes you want to keep on and on, and to go much farther than you know you ought to, or if you find it hard to stop; or if that's the main thing you think about when you're planning to go out somewhere with her—then I think it's smart to watch your step!

Question. Why do so many older girls keep telephoning you, and want you to take them to the movies, or buy them candy and cokes, or spend a lot of money on them when you haven't got a big allowance? Why can't they leave a fellow alone?

Answer. Well, of course there are some girls who feel that they can't get dates any other way. And of course there *are* fellows who are grafters and like to be invited to go places, especially if they are clever enough to make the girls pay for them! Some girls are willing to pay for boys who have no more pride than to be tame cats that way. This doesn't apply to the sensible plan of "going Dutch," which is perfectly all right, of course. And there are some girls who are uncomfortable when they are with older boys or men, and feel much more at ease with boys of your age.

Question. Some people say you can tell, by looking at a girl's face in some way, when she is menstruating. Is that true?

Answer. No—no more than it is true, as some people think, that you can tell by a boy's face whether or not he masturbates. Both are silly ideas that have absolutely no truth in them.

Question. I've been told that those long-drawn-out kisses, longer even than those you see in the movies, can cause a girl to have a baby. Is that true?

Answer. No, except that such kisses may excite the boy and the girl and lead them to do other things that may end up with the girl's having a baby! That's why that sort of kissing, and the other things that are just as exciting, had better be put off until after folks are married, when having a baby is what most people want. Having a baby before marriage is something that can and frequently does ruin a girl's chances for happiness, for the rest of her life. And it can stop a boy's chances for any more education and future advancement, if as sometimes happens he is forced into marrying her.

Question. What is an abortion? And wouldn't that save them both from the sort of trouble you speak of?

Answer. Unfortunately, no. In the first place, an abortion, which means destroying the life of the fetus, or embryo, or infant before it comes out of the mother's womb and into the world, is a crime for which there is serious punishment. Then too it is so dangerous that it may ruin a girl's health, make her sterile (so that she can't ever have a baby) or even kill her outright. So you see that the cure is worse than the disease!

"After all, fellows," as the doctor ended his talk and started for the door, "there's a lot of satisfaction in being decent, and a good sport, and having the feeling toward girls and women we all know the right sort of boys and men have. We know they're not as strong as we are and so are entitled to our protection; and it just isn't cricket to harm them or make trouble for them. And that's what immorality does—it degrades.

"There are lots of ways of having good times with girls. Let's not choose the wrong ones," and the doctor slipped out the door and got into his car.

DOCTOR, CAN YOU TELL ME?

JUST AS THE DOCTOR WAS ABOUT TO SLAM THE CAR DOOR, one of the boys who had crowded around, and who seemed most interested but had asked no questions, ran up to the car door and asked:

"Can you give me a lift, Doctor?"

"Sure, jump in." The doctor slammed the door, and they rode for a minute or two without speaking. Then the boy broke the silence:

"Doctor, there's something that's been bothering me a lot lately. I think I must be terribly vicious, or rotten, or something. For whenever I see some of these pictures in magazines on the newsstands of women without much on in the way of clothes, or when I hear the other guys talking about the dames they've done things with, my mind gets to working, and I think all sorts of smutty things.

"I know I oughtn't to do this. But somehow I can't seem to help it. I know I ought to have a strong enough will to make myself think right thoughts, not wrong ones. But somehow or other, the more I try to stop having these thoughts, the more I keep on, and the worse it gets. Why am I so different from other guys who are clean-minded? Why can't I make my mind stay as clean as theirs?"

They rode in silence for two or three minutes. Then the doctor remarked quietly:

"You're not one bit different from most of the rest of us, Don. It's perfectly natural and normal for you to begin to have mental images starting up, after looking at these suggestive pictures or hearing smutty talk. There would probably be something to worry about, if you didn't.

"It's this almost universal male tendency to have sexual thoughts that makes writers and editors of books and magazines play up the sexy side of life and exaggerate it in pictures and type. Folks want to sell what they make; and writers and publishers are no different from other people in this respect.

"But there's something a lot worse than this. You've probably heard that there's a several-million-dollar business based on the publication and sale of what is known as 'pornographic material.' What we used to call 'French post cards' have been blown up into a vast, disreputable, and criminal industry whose purpose is to make lots of money by debauching young people. The government is doing its best to run this to earth and stamp it out. But it crops up again and again."

"Yeah, I know," answered Don. "Some of the fellows in school pass these filthy pictures around. I've even known them to show them to nice girls, though they're more likely to show them to girls they know aren't too particular. They get me to thinking these crummy thoughts, too, though I know I oughtn't to."

"Don," said the doctor earnestly, "the next time anything of this sort turns up, and you get to thinking these thoughts,

I'd like you to do your best to make yourself remember two things. The first is that while you can't do one single thing to keep the birds from flying in the sky over your head, you certainly don't have to let them light there, mess up your hair, and even build their nests there!

"You can't stop them from flying over your head. The upper air is free, and no matter what silly things you might do to try to stop them, you couldn't. So you let them fly, and pay no attention to them.

"The other thing I'd like you to remember is that there is no such thing as a 'psychological negative.' Sounds very technical, doesn't it? But in reality it's very simple. Let me give you an example of what it means.

"Suppose I were to say to you, 'Now don't think about the end of your nose. Whatever else you do, *don't think about the end of your nose!* Now, remember what I say, Don, *you must not think about the end of your nose!!!'*

"You'd probably tell me, if you were not too polite, 'Well, if you'll only stop telling me not to think about it, I won't. But as long as you keep telling me *not* to think about it, and as long as I keep trying *not* to think about it, I simply can't help thinking about it.'

"That's what is meant by the law, 'There is no such thing as a psychological negative.' You cannot 'not think' about something. All you can do is to think about something else. So don't be worried if these smutty thoughts keep flying over your head. Don't waste a minute trying to 'not think' about them. Just think about something else.

"One thing more," the doctor emphasized firmly. "Don't let yourself think for one moment that you have a dirty mind, or that there must be something wrong about you because you sometimes 'think unclean thoughts.' I have them, too,

Don, and so does every other normal boy or man, though not everyone will admit it. You're perfectly normal in this respect, just like most of the rest of us. So quit 'low rating' yourself.

"Just one thing more. Whenever you happen to see any boy passing these dirty pictures around, go at once to your teacher or your principal, your pastor or your doctor, or come to me if you want to, and tell what you have seen. No, that's not 'tale-bearing,' or 'snitching,' or tattling. It's just being a good citizen and helping the government get this mental garbage removed to where it can't contaminate decent people."

"But what ought a guy to do when someone begins to tell smutty stories? I can't seem to bring myself to tell them they shouldn't. That looks too 'goody goody,' or like the 'holier than thou' attitude I've read about."

"Neither can I," replied the doctor. "But what you can do, and I can too, is to show pretty plainly, without saying one word, that you don't think that sort of crummy talk is either funny or clever. Don't think for a moment that your example doesn't count. You can be one of the fellows who set a standard of decency in your school. I'd hate to be known, as I've known folks to be, as a guy with a whole string of dirty jokes. That's the sort of a rep I don't want any part of."

They rode on without further discussion until the doctor drew up in front of his office, when Don said:

"Before you go in, Doctor, there's one thing more I'd like to ask you about. It's this business of cheating in school. Almost everyone seems to be doing it, so maybe it's not so terrible. But it gets a guy into a lot of trouble if the teacher finds it out. And besides, I know, way down deep inside me, that it is *not* all right.

"I'm still scared it will come out somehow that I cheated on our last final exams. I know you won't blab, so I can tell you the truth about it. I'm sure I'm no worse than most of the rest of the class. But I can't help feeling that I'm doing wrong when I get help from someone else. What ought I to do about it?" And he looked relieved, now that he had made a clean breast of what it was that had been bothering him.

The doctor sat thinking, while the motor idled. Then he turned off the ignition and began, thoughtfully:

"You've opened up a big problem. The school authorities have never solved it, and I'm sure you and I can't find the answer either. But it *is* something you have to settle for yourself. And maybe I can help you think it through.

"If I were you, I'd figure out a line of conduct for myself. That was what I did when I was your age and was worried over what seemed to me to be the almost universal custom among my classmates of looking at the other guy's paper, or passing notes from one to the other when the teacher wasn't looking.

"I made up my mind to do what I knew was the honest thing and not get mixed up with something I knew was wrong, even though it did seem to be done pretty constantly. Nobody ever seemed to feel that I thought I was 'holier than thou.' But the others knew I didn't either ask or give help, so I wasn't bothered. It sure made school a lot pleasanter to have a good conscience, instead of always having a guilty conscience and wondering when things would come to the surface and trouble would start for everyone.

"It will help you over a lot of uncomfortable times, Don, if you'll try to bear this one thing in mind. Like everyone else, and especially like everyone around your age, you are inclined to be in a good deal of doubt about yourself. Even folks that appear to others to be 'stuck on themselves' aren't as a rule too certain of themselves. So they try extra hard to make everyone else think they are tops. They wouldn't do that if they felt certain that they were. It's that old 'inferiority reaction' or 'inferiority complex' that folks talk so much about."

"That's quite a new idea to me," replied Don, thoughtfully. "But I believe you're right. That *is* what's the matter with me. But what can a guy do to get over that feeling?"

"I don't suppose we ever get over it completely," answered the doctor. "And maybe it's just as well that we don't. But if you will try to stop analyzing yourself and thinking about your feeling all the time and get out instead with other people and take an active part in what is going on, you can keep this inferiority feeling from getting you down.

"So glad you felt like talking these things over with me. You know I'm your friend, and I'm never too busy to chat with you. Drop around any time you get up against something that bothers you."

Both got out, and they parted at the doctor's door.

"Thanks a million, Doctor. You've sure answered my questions, and you've made me feel a lot better." And the lad heaved a deep breath, as if he'd had a load lifted from his chest.

"Come back with more questions any time you feel like it. I may not have all the answers, but I'll do the best I can." The doctor thrust his key into the door latch while Don walked slowly down the street.

THE RACE MUST GO ON

THE NEXT TIME THE DOCTOR CAME TO SCHOOL, HE FELT like quite an old hand; and the boys, knowing what to expect in the way of a discussion, were all ready to go. They were not disappointed. The doctor came directly to the point.

I promised you the first day I talked with you that I'd tell you how the male elements, or sperms, leave the body of the boy or man. Now that seems a simple enough thing to do, but it really packs quite a punch for it opens up almost everything that worries a boy who hasn't had these things explained to him fully and clearly. That's exactly what I'm going to do for you fellows today. If there's anything I've skipped over or haven't explained clearly and you haven't nerve enough to ask me about it, it's your funeral, not mine. All I can do is promise to tell you everything you want to know. So here's the low-down.

The first way that the semen, the fluid containing the male elements, leaves the body is by means of what are properly called "nocturnal emissions," because they take place at night, during sleep. Boys usually call them "wet dreams." There are so many mistaken ideas about these, and what causes them, and these ideas worry boys so, that I want you to know just what they are and what they mean.

You remember I told you that the testicles make these sperms and store them in the body, floating about in a thick whitish fluid called semen. Whenever the storage tanks get too full, they empty themselves. Sometimes they do this at night, when a boy is dreaming about sex matters. Sometimes they do it without any sign at all except that the night clothing or bed clothes may be wet or discolored. This may happen several nights in succession, or as seldom as several weeks apart, or in some boys hardly ever.

Do these do any harm? No indeed—unless a boy doesn't understand how perfectly harmless they are, and worries over them, especially if he thinks that they are his fault. If he is told that they come because of so-called "impure thoughts" he may have had, he should not believe it for it's not so. Every normal boy has such thoughts at times; and they do no harm as long as he doesn't brood over them and keep thinking about them. And whether he does or not they have absolutely nothing to do with noctural emissions, which are just as natural and normal for a boy to have as menstruation is for a girl. They are a helpful safety valve. Nothing he can do can prevent them, fortunately; for that might be like tying down the safety valve on an engine.

But they *can* do a great deal of harm if a fellow is foolish enough to listen to ignorant or crooked advisers, or if he happens to see and believe some of the advertisements that used to be commonly seen in public rest rooms. It is surprising how many a Joe you'd think would have more sense, falls for this stuff and proves to be a soft touch for some advertising quack who tells him that these are "draining away his manhood"—whatever that may mean!

Is there anything at all to that kind of mullarky? Absolutely none at all—take my word for it. So if any of you fellows have been worrying that you were being harmed by these dreams, or that you must be dirty minded or you wouldn't have them and the thoughts that sometimes go along with them after you wake up, stop worrying.

Above all, don't let anybody take you for a ride, and get money out of you on the false claim that he can "cure" you, by exercises or medicine. You can't cure someone who's well already! And if that's all that's the matter with you, you sure are very well indeed!

Now there is another way in which the semen, or seminal fluid, can leave the body, and sometimes does. This is from something that I suppose every normal boy that ever lived in this world has done, some time or other. And that is rubbing or handling his penis until it causes a pleasant sensation that is usually followed by the forcible ejection of some whitish fluid, which of course is the semen we've been talking about. And this, which has been given the name of masturbation, is something about which there's been more misinformation and pure bunk than any other thing I can think of at the moment.

It's perfectly natural that every boy at some time or other should discover a pleasant sensation could be had by doing just this very thing. He may find it out by himself by accident; he may be told and shown about it by other fellows of the wrong sort who enjoy getting younger boys into trouble, and exerting power over them through fear of exposure.

Any boy knows by instinct that this is something he ought not to do; but it is pleasant, and so he keeps on doing it, but tries to keep it a dead secret. Sooner or later someone finds out about it; and then the trouble starts!

If it happens to be the boy's father or mother who makes the "awful" discovery, and they have the usual mistaken ideas about its seriousness, they'll probably be terribly worried and think that he's contracted a habit that is going to harm him for life. They may accuse him as thought it were some terrible thing he is guilty of. Or maybe they'll go in deep shame and embarrassment to their doctor and confess that their son is guilty of such an awful thing that they can hardly force themselves to mention it even in the strictest confidence.

It's surprising how difficult it often is for a doctor to convince these good people that what their son has been doing is not some dreadfully shameful act, but simply what probably every boy has done. The very fact that in all probability the father himself did it when he was a boy, and of course got over the habit as every normal person does, makes him just that much more indignant and frightened and critical, all the same time, about his own boy.

The doctor will be doing the whole family—father, mother, and son—the greatest service if he can convince them of the truth of what I've just been telling you. That is that it's nothing at all to worry over; and that the sooner they and the boy realize this reassuring fact—and it *is* a fact I can assert without fear of contradiction—the sooner he'll master the habit and leave it behind him, just as he leaves all his other kid habits behind him.

In fact, I've found that one of the most helpful things I can do is to tell them on my word of honor that it's not much more serious than thumb sucking! Of course no one would want a boy to go on sucking his thumb till he grew to be a man. But we certainly don't feel that it's a family disgrace that a boy used to suck his thumb. He got over the one childhood habit—and he'll get over this other one, if he is not badgered and heckled and everlastingly scared into continually thinking about it, and the awful results he's been told will follow it. That's the surest way in the world to make him continue the habit.

We come now to the third and most important way the male elements can leave the man's body. This is by intercourse. The purpose of this, as you can see from what we've been talking about, is for a sperm to unite with an ovum to form an embryo that will eventually grow into another man or woman.

Now there are two entirely different ways in which this can take place. The one way is natural, normal, and right. The other way is wrong, and always brings trouble of some sort or other as a result.

The first way is marriage. Here a man and a woman choose each other over everybody else in the whole world, just as your own father and mother did, and promise to live together and make a home for themselves and the children they may bring into the world. This is the natural way, the purpose for which sex was provided.

But there is another way, that is called by the long name, "promiscuity," or better, immorality. Here two people, without either love or respect for each other and without any wish to bring children into the world, have intercourse. This way is unlawful, dangerous, and terribly selfish.

It is unlawful because it is forbidden by God's law and by the teachings of all religions. It is dangerous, because it frequently causes serious disease. And it is selfish, because in spite of precautions and so-called preventives, it so often brings into the world an innocent baby who has to go through life with the undeserved shame of being known as illegitimate, or a bastard.

I've given you a long enough lecture for today. No, you needn't applaud. I'll take your word for it that you weren't bored!

The doctor smiled as the boys shuffled their feet and started for the doors.

WHAT? STILL MORE QUESTIONS

IN SPITE OF PROF'S SUGGESTION THAT THE DOCTOR DO AS the boys wanted him to do, and run over into the next period, he shook his head, saying simply:

"You fellows have had enough of my talking for one day. If any of you can take any more, come on down here in front and I'll answer anything that you ask me. Then we can get on down to the lunchroom before everything is gone."

Most of the boys crowded out through the doors; but several of the older boys came down to the front and milled about as one of their number addressed the doctor:

Question. You haven't told us how the sperms get from where they're made, in the testicles, to outside of the body. Just how do they get out?

Answer. Well, as you say, they're formed in the testicles. A tube with muscular walls, called the vas deferens, runs from each testicle to one of the seminal vesicles. These are reservoirs or storage vats for the semen that the vas deferens sends along to them. When these become full, they empty themselves through another long stretch of the vas deferens, into a tube called the urethra.

Question. The urethra? Isn't that the tube that runs through the penis and carries off the urine? Why doesn't that get mixed with the sperms in the semen?

Answer. Because there's a little valve on the bladder that closes whenever the semen is being expelled, so that no urine can leave the bladder until the semen has gone through.

Question. Isn't a boy likely to lose his manhood if he doesn't use these parts of the body you've been telling us about? I've always heard that if you tied up a leg or put an arm in a splint for too long a time, the muscles would wither and become weak and useless because they weren't used. Why wouldn't this happen if a person never had intercourse so as to exercise these organs?

Answer. Because the different systems, male and female, are being "used" actively all the time, in the ways I've been telling you about. The boy's make sperms and "testosterone," the male juice or "hormone." The girl's make ova (eggs) and "estrogen," the female hormone. There's no danger of their withering away from disuse, as a muscle would. A boy who doesn't have intercourse is storing up his manhood, just as a person stores up money in the bank, instead of wasting it.

Question. But I've read that if a boy or girl gets all worked up and excited by petting or reading hot stories or seeing sexy pictures or watching a strip tease at a show, and doesn't have intercourse to relieve himself, he gets terribly "frustrated"—whatever that means! Isn't that true? If it isn't so, then some pretty well-known authors are lying; for they write as if that was something everyone admitted.

Answer. Don't fall for everything you see in print. Lots of folks make statements it would be hard for them to prove. It may "frustrate" me (make me feel baffled and unhappy, that is) if I see another doctor driving a Lincoln or a Cadillac, or living in a mansion on millionaire's row, or making some wonderful scientific discovery. But that doesn't excuse me if I steal a car or rob a bank so as to have what I want so badly. Instead, I'll land in the jailhouse.

But if my desire to have these things makes me work harder to get them than I otherwise would, then instead of being made unhappy by not having them, I may be spurred on to work harder so that I can earn them for myself. In the very same way, the fact that a boy or girl doesn't snatch at the questionable pleasure of intercourse (and believe me, many a boy and girl who've grabbed at it in this hasty wrong way have found it a long way from pleasurable) may make them willing to work and wait and earn the real pleasure of marriage.

Question. What about one of the older fellows in the senior class who's always sounding off about the girls he's "made" who've never fallen for anyone before?

Answer. He tries to make other fellows think he's a hot shot. That shows that he feels shaky about himself and has to build himself up in that cheap way—the only way he can beat the decent fellows. The rest of you know him for the louse he is.

Question. What is circumcision?

Answer. It's cutting off a small layer or fold of skin that covers the glans, or end of the penis. It's a religious rite for some people, and a means of insuring cleanliness for some others.

Question. We used to josh one boy in our gym class who had such a long foreskin he was ashamed to take a shower where the other fellows could see him. Why was he so different from the rest of us?

Answer. That small difference meant nothing at all. But fellows are pretty cruel, or at least mighty thoughtless, the way they make fun of anyone who's the least bit different from the average. If such a foreskin is tight, as well as long, it might be wise for him to be circumcised so that he could keep himself clean more easily. But that is something for his doctor to advise him about.

Question. If, as you say, it isn't necessary to use these parts so as to develop them, why would anyone buy something I saw advertised that was guaranteed to increase their size?

Answer. It isn't necessary. As I told you before the size of these parts has nothing whatever to do with a fellow's manliness or "virility," as it's sometimes called.

Question. What I can't understand is what makes older fellows, and sometimes even men that you'd think were decent people, try to get boys to let them do things to them that they know they ought not to.

Answer. If anybody of that sort ever gets to fooling around with you, or with any boys you know, don't be sucker enough to fall for it or let them get away with it. Don't hesitate for one minute to tell someone in authority exactly what has happened, or what you have seen or know. No matter how fine a man he seems to be, or how respected he is in the community, any man who tries to get you to undress, or to let him play with you ought to be shown up for what he is. If it happens around school, go to Prof. Or if it's some boys' club worker as sometimes happens, go to your minister or your Sunday School teacher or superintendent. Or tell your father, or come to me, or go to any older man you have confidence in, and spill it all. You'll be protecting other younger boys as well as yourself, to say nothing of putting such a crumb where he will be protected from himself. For the law takes a very dim view of that sort of monkey business.

Question. But why would anyone want to do anything like that?

Answer. It would take too long to tell you why some men get their satisfaction out of ruining young boys, and getting them started doing the same sort of thing with other youngsters. They are mentally "off," of course; and they really ought to be taken away for treatment, and kept where they can't do any more harm. But until the world wakes up to the fact that such people are dangerous, and keeps them separated from the rest of us, you fellows must help locate them.

Question. But won't they say you're a tattle tale, or a sissy, or a poor sport, or a spy, if you do that?

Answer. Do you call a plainclothesman, or an F.B.I. agent, or an underground revolutionist in a country behind the Iron Curtain, a poor sport? That sort of thing takes a lot more guts than almost anything I know of; and men get pretty important citations and decorations for going beyond the call of duty that way. The only way you can fight that kind of dirty undercover corruption that Tom speaks of, is with the counter-fire of good common sense and fine citizenship.

If you saw a crook snatching a purse, or a second story man entering the house of one of your friends, you'd send in an alarm for the police, wouldn't you? Sure, you would. So don't fall for any such false reasoning from a man or a crowd who are doing more harm, much more, to young boys who can't speak up for themselves, than anybody who lifts a purse or burglarizes a house. *They're* the ones who are the poorest sort of poor sports. They know that the only way they can be stopped and exposed is by the good sportsmanship of anybody who finds out what they are up to.

TOM, JIM . . . AND BILL

THE DOCTOR'S DOORBELL RANG A FEW DAYS LATER. HE went to the door and let in two boys, Tom and Jim, who were evidently very much disturbed about something. Brought into the consulting room after the last patient had left, they started to speak, stopped, then tried again. Finally Tom blurted out:

"Doctor, is there anything we can do that will keep us from going crazy?"

The doctor guessed what had led to this question, for he had heard it asked several times before. It took a little cross questioning, however, before the boys would admit what had happened. The truth was that Tom's mother had suspected that he was handling his genital organs, and had told him in horrified tones that "the insane asylums are just full of people who have gone crazy because of such self-pollution." What made it worse was that she really believed it; and she was so certain about it and so upset, that the boys believed it too. Of course, Tom at once told Jim.

Both the boys had stayed awake the greater part of that night, and the next, too; and had brooded over the matter pretty steadily ever since. Then they heard the doctor talk in school; but hadn't gotten up courage to ask him about the matter. At last they couldn't stand it any longer, so they came to him in terror to find out if there was anything they could do to save them from this terrible end. They just couldn't believe what he had told them that day.

The answer he was able to give them was prompt, direct and reassuring. He explained that while the habit they had been indulging in was anything but a desirable one, and had once been considered even by doctors to be a very dangerous one, they had nothing to fear. He told them that it is now known to be a scientific fact that, while it is something to be discontinued, it is nothing to worry about, unless they were to carry it on into their later adult years. And he was sure that they had sense enough not to do that.

He told them, as he had told the fellows at school, that it was kid stuff, like thumb sucking, that most sensible fellows succeeded in stopping it when they realized what it was. To be sure, some of the patients in mental hospitals do indulge in the habit. But if they do, it's because they are already mentally unbalanced. They certainly never got that way as a result of masturbating. The belief that that was the cause of their mental condition is all poppycock.

The boys were plainly greatly relieved at what the doctor told them. But there was evidently something more that they hadn't quite gotten up their courage to mention. The doctor realized this; and after waiting for them to go on, he encouraged them:

"Come on, come on, get it off your chests. Come clean with whatever it is that's still eating on you. Let's get it all over with, now that we've gone so far."

After looking at each other to see which should speak first, Jim finally broke down and admitted what was still disturbing them:

"I guess I believe you when you say that most fellows get over this all right. But you see it's a little different in our case. We've both got 'lost manhood' as a result of what we've been doing for so long. And we haven't got enough money to pay the doctor to cure us, even if it wasn't too late to do anything for us."

"What doctor are you talking about?"

"Why, the one whose address was printed on the poster we saw on the wall of a men's rest room. It explained all about our trouble. It said that 'wet dreams' were a sure sign of 'lost manhood'; and it said for anyone who suffered from these 'night pollutions' to go to his office for treatment. If a fellow wasn't too far gone and could still be cured, he'd try to do what he could for him. Do you suppose there's any hope that he could cure us?"

"That crook is no doctor. He's just a quack, getting blood money from boys and men like yourselves who don't know that reputable physicians never advertise. As I told you the other day, the 'self abuse' and 'secret vice' and 'self pollution' the ad tells about are all silly old-fashioned names that were used when people thought this bad habit caused all sorts of dreadful things.

"For even if a fellow should slip and give way to it, some time he'll overcome it.

"I believe you've stopped the habit. So forget all about it. And forget too all the terrible effects you've been reading and hearing about; for I can assure you you'll never suffer from any of them.

"I wish all the boys and men who are terrified by this sort of dirty advertising had the good sense to talk to someone who knows the score. That would break up this racket. Good night." The doctor led the relieved boys to the door.

As he opened it to let them out, and they started down the front steps toward the street, they saw a boy looking up at them from the foot of the steps. He was somewhat older than Tom or Jim; and the light from the front door showed his pale face and greatly worried expression.

"Sorry, Bill, we waited for you at the corner, but it's too late now," exclaimed Tom, plainly very much disappointed.

"Not a bit of it. Come on in," and the doctor herded them into the dark hall and back to the inner office, switching on his desk light so that it shone on his own face, instead of on theirs, which were thus left in shadow. This made it easier for them to explain the situation. Tom began at once:

"Bill was going to meet us, but he didn't make it. You see he's got a bad disease, and he's sure it's one that it will take years to cure, if it can be cured at all, which he doubts. How can he go about finding out?"

"What makes him so sure?"

"Well, he's been running around with some of the older men, 'cause he thinks he's too old to be going with us. At least he did think so until last week, when they all went to a beer joint that Bill knew had a bad rep, and hung around with some girls he knew weren't the right sort. After they had bought some drinks, one of them let him spend the night with her in a rooming house near by; and today he's sure he's got a bad disease as a result of what he did."

During all this time, Bill had sat silent, his face in the shadow. The doctor got to his feet, slipped his arm casually about his shoulders, and remarked in a matter of fact tone as he walked toward the door:

"Let's come into the examining room, Bill, and see for sure," and the doctor and Bill disappeared through the open door which closed behind them, leaving Tom and Jim nervously waiting for the bad news they were sure would come out of the room.

It took but a few minutes questioning and a brief but careful examination for the doctor to discover that Bill's imagination, reinforced by a bad conscience, had run away with him and resulted in his making a serious false diagnosis of his condition by exaggerating a few imaginary symptoms. Opening the door of the examining room, he led Bill back to where his friends were anxiously waiting for him. Leaning back in his big leather chair, he told them what he'd discovered.

A blister that had come on Bill's lip after kissing the girl, and that he thought was a syphilitic primary sore or chancre, had proved to be nothing more serious than a cold sore. And the rash on his face was simply an aggravation of a long-standing acne, such as had brought Jack to the doctor at the beginning of our story.

"Bill's in better luck than he has any right to expect," announced the doctor. "There are two very serious diseases, and one other that's not so serious but is terribly painful and annoying, that are frequently caught as the result of monkey business that Bill engaged in that night last week."

"I'm not going to burden you with an account of all the symptoms, for that would take us half the night. If you care to learn what they are, I'll give you a little Government pamphlet that explains all about them. Next time—if there *is* a next time, for I sure hope and believe that Bill has brains enough to take this as a danger sign and lay off any future playing with dynamite—he might not be quite so lucky."

"But the older men I went there with told me that there were certain sure-fire precautions you could take that would protect you one hundred per cent against these diseases.

What's more, they said that the same precautions would make it sure that a baby wouldn't come from what you were doing."

"Well, Bill, when they told you that hundred per cent yarn, they were getting pretty careless about their figures. There *are* certain precautions that a man can take; and they sometimes work. But they are a long way from perfect, or sure-fire, or one hundred per cent effective."

"As far as that goes, even such an apparently simple thing as kissing a girl who has one of these diseases and who doesn't show it—and these diseases are of very common occurrence among both men and women who do the things your pals were doing, and succeeded in getting you to do—can give you either of the two most serious ones. There is only one one hundred per cent way to protect yourself—and that is to steer clear of that sort of folks entirely."

Bill let out a long breath that showed his relief, and sank back in his chair. But Tom, who had followed all this with the closest attention, plainly had something that was worrying him. The doctor noticed his hesitating manner, and turned toward him, with the air of one who was determined to get it all over with, if it took all night:

"You're next, Tom, so don't lose your turn."

Thus directly appealed to, Tom resolutely took his courage in both hands, and blurted out:

"What's this graveyard stuff that's been going around about one of the girls being taken out of school because she's going to have a baby?"

"Hasn't she been running with a fast crowd—a crowd that you'd hate to see your sister going with?"

"Well, yes, perhaps, though I know my sister would give her favorite compact if they'd take her in. They come from some of the best families in town."

"But that doesn't make them the best boys and girls in town by a long shot. You know that, Jim, and so does everyone else in school. Now if you want to know what's happened, I'll tell you. If you remember what we said about how sperms leave a boy's body, you'll recall that one of the ways was what they call intercourse. This is all right when it happens between people who have fallen in love and gotten married. For that's the way the population of the world is kept up and actually increased year by year.

"But when it takes place between people who are not married, and who don't love each other, but are just 'out for a thrill,' it's something else again. for many reasons. The first is that it exposes both of them to very painful, serious, sometimes disgusting illnesses called venereal diseases—ask Bill whether he doesn't think this is reason enough to lay off that sort of stuff. But worse still—worse, because it's so rotten unfair—is the unwanted pregnancy that comes in spite of the precautions they told Bill were so sure. It's unfair because the girl gets so much worse a deal out of it than the boy does—though his share can be bad enough, if he has any decency at all about him.

"I needn't tell you what such a thing means to a girl. She is disgraced throughout the community, sometimes thrown out by her family, set aside as no longer fit for a decent man to marry. The boy who has caused all this must feel pretty terrible, even if it never comes out that he is the father of the child. For he has ruined the life and future prospects of a girl who was no more at fault than he was. Worst of all he has helped to send out into the world a poor little innocent kid that the law brands as illegitimate."

"But that's not justice," protested one of the boys.

"Who said it was just? I didn't—in fact, I just told you how rottenly unjust it is. But that's the way the world is set up, like it or not; and neither one person, nor yet a thousand who think they know better and would like to change things, can make it any different. So if you want to know who's really a poor sport, and about as low a louse as walks the earth, it's the fellow who does that miserable cowardly thing to a girl for a few minutes or hours of so-called pleasure.

"Now let's shut up shop and get home and to bed, the whole lot of us. Glad you fellows felt like coming in and getting things straightened out. It reminds me of the days when I had a gang of Boy Scouts coming to the house to talk things over with the Scoutmaster; and later on, in the Army, when I was a Medical Officer and had to discuss these things with the men and officers in my command. It always helps to get things out into the open, instead of keeping them shut up and festering inside you.

"And Bill, you've had a very valuable lesson, for free, take it from me. Next time you feel like taking a chance, remember how you felt between the time you had your fun—if you call it fun—and the time I told you you were okay and wouldn't have to pay for it this time. Then remember how good it felt to know that you were safe. It's worth thinking about, Bill. Goodnight!" and the boys walked off together, leaving the doctor to wonder how deep what he had been saying would sink in and bring the kind of results he hoped for.

SPEEDING, AND BRAKES

"HAVE YOU SEEN DOC'S NEW CAR?" ASKED JIM, AS HE AND Tom were passing the doctor's office. Just then the door opened to let out a patient; and the doctor, seeing the boys admiring his new car, beckoned them to come in.

"So you finally broke down and got that new bus, didn't you?" remarked Jim, as they entered the office. "It must have been a supersalesman that persuaded you to turn in that faithful elderly contraption of yours."

"Yes, I must admit that he did do a little high pressure selling," conceded the doctor. "But if you think *he* was good, you should see the fuel salesman who's been trying to persuade me to use something they mix with the gas and grease. According to what he says, it must be the world's best."

"What does he claim for it?" asked the boys curiously.

"Well, for one thing, it makes the car go faster, so you can have a lot more fun with it. And it makes riding very much pleasanter and more comfortable, because you don't feel the bumps in the road. He says that many of the best people in town have been using it."

"Then what are you waiting for?" asked Jim. If it's that good, I should think everybody would be using it."

"Lots of folks are. And he certainly makes out a good case for his product. But while I was being tempted to fall for his line, it suddenly occurred to me that there must be a gimmick in it somewhere. And sure enough when I got him backed into a corner, he had to admit that there was one serious drawback and a few others that are nearly as bad."

"What was the big disadvantage?" the boys wanted to know.

"Why, it seems that the stuff somehow weakens your brakes so that they don't act quite so promptly, nor so efficiently, either. Then, too, if you once get used to using it, it's pretty hard to give it up; and the longer you use it, the more expensive it gets!"

"That sounds like a fairly long list of drawbacks," pondered Tom slowly. "Especially that business about the brakes. Would you dare to drive a car that didn't have a number one braking system?"

"Oh, I don't know as that means so much," replied the doctor. "He says some of the most careful and sensible men in town use it. If they can get by with it, why shouldn't I be able to? Besides, if you have more fun driving at the higher speeds it gives, why are the brakes so important?" and the doctor looked as if he wanted to be fair and hear both sides of the argument.

Both boys stared at him for almost a full minute. Their faces showed blank amazement. Finally Tom broke the silence.

"I don't mean any disrespect, doctor, honestly I don't. But you talk, to me, like someone who is slightly balmy. Do you actually expect us to believe that you, or any other sensible driver, would put a higher octane gas in your car, and at the same time weaken its braking equipment? I wonder if the salesman is telling the truth when he claims that sensible business men are mixing the stuff with their gas? I wouldn't drive round the block with you if I knew you had any of that bug juice in your tank. Would you, Jim?"

Jim gazed at the doctor thoughtfully, then shook his head in an emphatic negative, and spoke his mind forcefully.

"I don't want to hurt your feelings, Doc. But I wouldn't drive with you, or the most dependable driver I ever knew, who would do that fool stunt. I just wouldn't take that chance."

"I feel sure you *have* taken that chance, though, both of you, and many times too. And unless I am greatly mistaken, you'll do it a great many more times. I certainly hope you won't buy any of the stuff yourselves, though. And I hope the time may come when all of us will have sense enough not to use it, nor ride with people who do. Apparently, though, we are still a long way off from that good day."

"I can't believe the Government would allow such stuff to be sold," objected Jim stubbornly. "Why, it would be like carrying dynamite around on the public highway."

"But the Government does allow it. You see, they take in a lot of money on the tax, which is much higher than that on either plain or premium gas. I'll admit that lots of people think the Government could get its revenues in a lot of safer and more respectable ways. Still, they go on passing out the stuff just the same."

Suddenly Tom, who had been frowning perplexedly, broke into a loud horse laugh. Slapping Jim vigorously on the back, he shouted, "Haw, I get it. How about you, Jim, old Scout?"

"What do you mean, 'you get it'? What do you get?"

"Wake up and think, Stoopid. What do all the pious folks tell drivers not to mix with gasoline? What is it that makes driving more fun after you've drunk some of it? And what slows down your reflexes, so that you can't tramp down on your brakes so quick? Come alive, Bird Brain," and Tom poked his friend vigorously in the ribs again.

"Well, I'm not going to preach a temperance sermon at you. But let's see if I've made any false claims about it. Let's take up the points one by one, and you can call me if I make a single statement that can't be proved by a dozen school text books and medical volumes, as well as pamphlets on safe driving.

"Alcohol, even the little bit there is in a cocktail or a glass of beer, slows down your judgment while it speeds up your emotions. So you drive faster but much less carefully. By slowing down your reflexes it lengthens the time it takes to apply brakes. It gets more expensive the longer you use it, because you get to taking more and more of it; and it's mighty hard to quit it when once you get used to it. And you know as well as I do that not all the sensible business and professional men in town are on the wagon, though a lot of folks honestly believe the time will come when they'll have to get on board, or else stop driving while they drink.

"Remember, too, I'm not talking about drunken driving. It's the 'small one' that does all these dangerous things to the person who's driving, and thinks he's as good as he is when he hasn't had that potent little bit of alcohol. You certainly have to admit that the Government does make a tidy sum taxing the stuff; though whether or not it's clear profit would take an accountant who would tot up injuries and deaths it causes as against the financial intake.

"But now that I've sold you my bill of goods, let's switch to one other thing about my magic juice. I mean what even a little bit of liquor, or even beer, does to the boy and girl after they've parked their car on a soft shoulder. Their emotions are heightened while their braking power (inhibitions, the psychologist calls the good common sense that tells us to stop when we've gone far enough) is weakened. I don't need to tell you fellows that that adds up to a mighty dangerous combination.

"So think about what I've told you, next time you are taking a girl home from a party—especially if the lady of the house doesn't know what I've been talking about, and has spiked the punch."

"You sure played us for suckers, Doc. You shouldn't have taken advantage of our tender years and your wisdom that has come from all the long years you've lived and charged people for your advice. That wasn't quite cricket, you know," and Tom looked doubtful, as though uncertain whether to kick himself, or reproach the doctor further.

"I'm sorry, fellows, honestly I am, and I humbly apologize. But you did look so trustful and so interested in my newly discovered devil juice that I just couldn't resist the temptation. But g'by now; here comes a patient," and the doctor walked over to one door as the boys slipped out through the other.

UNDERSTANDING YOURSELF

THE DOCTOR WAS TAKING HIS WEEKLY AFTERNOON OFF. He had invited his five friends to go along with him to the lake to try out his new speed boat and do a little fishing. Jim and Tom were working; but the others eagerly accepted.

The doctor had asked Harry to steer, so that he could lie back in the after cockpit and relax. Just then something happened that completely killed any idea of relaxation he might have been indulging.

Another boat coming up from astern had tooted a raucous horn and then tried to cut across their bow. But the other skipper hadn't counted on Harry's adroitness, and still less on his quick temper. The angry boy jabbed the throttle wide open, and shot ahead with a sudden burst of speed that threw his shipmates into a forcible huddle and banged Bill's head against Jack's with a resounding thump.

They barely cleared the other boat, but in doing so just missed crashing through her shiny mahogany planking. Luckily for them all, Harry was able to get their own transom clear of the other's bow, but with what looked like hardly an inch margin. The other skipper cursed them heartily as he rocked in their wake.

"I bet he won't try that one again," chortled Harry, turning to the doctor for approval. Instead he met a cool level look that pulled him up short. A look from the doctor always meant more to the boys than a tongue lashing from anyone else. So Harry at once launched into a defense of what he had done, winding up with:

"But you don't believe in a person's standing up for his rights, do you, sir?"

The doctor listened in silence until he had finished; then replied quietly,

"Stow it, Harry. I'd hoped maybe you'd grown up in this one respect, after your latest narrow squeak last week. But I guess you're one of those 'accident prone' people—the folks who never do grow up, when it comes to driving or sailing. There are lots of men, yes and women too, who are just kids when it comes to asserting their rights to the right of way.

"One of the things I'd hoped to talk to you fellows about at school was this business of understanding yourselves and what it is that makes you tick. I wanted to talk to you about the toughest job in the world—one that everybody has to learn to do, sooner or later, if he wants to save himself a lot of unnecessary grief.

"That job is learning to understand yourself, now that this change from boy into man has started."

"Well, take the wheel yourself, if you think I'm too much of a kid to be trusted with this new battleship of yours. But honest, Doc, I won't do that fool trick again, or any other one either, I promise you, if you do let me keep on with her. But whether you do or not, I'd like to hear just what you would have told us at school, if there'd been time.

"We've still got most of the afternoon before us; and I'll keep her down to a comfortable pace, with no spasms of speed to teach other folks manners. That'll give us plenty of time."

Jack, who'd been wondering how the doctor would handle Harry's weakness as well as some others of his own, rubbed his aching forehead, and sat up alertly to listen; while Bill called back from where he was sitting in the bow:

"Don't pull any punches when you get round to my part of the sermon, Doc. I've told both Harry and Jack what a fool I made of myself the other night, and what I told you and what you told me. I can take anything; so don't mind my feelings."

"Right-o, then; carry on, Harry. We don't mind swimming to shore if we have to, just to prove what a devil of a man you are," and the doctor grinned as Harry winced at the dig he knew he had earned. "Let's forget it. But I would like to tell you—"

"Excuse me, Doc. But can you really tell me why do you suppose it is that I do these fool stunts," interrupted Harry. "I swear every time I won't do this sort of thing again—and I mean it at the time. But I get so cussing mad when someone tries to put one over on me, that it seems as if I just *have* to show him that I'm as good as he is—and maybe just a little bit better!" and Harry unconsciously shrugged back his shoulders and sat up a little bit straighter as he remembered how he had wiped the other fellow's eye by his sudden tack and spurt.

"Why, Harry, you've just told us why; but not by your words. It's your actions that give you away," laughed the doctor. "You don't realize it; but you're just like every other Joe your age in not feeling quite sure how good you are. That means that you have to take every chance you get to show what a man you are! And you underline this thing you're not sure of, by sticking out your chest and straightening your back, as you did just now.

"No, I don't mean that you want to show *me.* It's the other fellows, as well as yourself, you've got to prove it to. By the time you get to be my age, you'll know perfectly well that you are not so hot, as every one does sooner or later who isn't a stuffed shirt who's succeeded in fooling himself. And by that time you'll realize what a waste of time it is to try to convince yourself and your pals of something you know just isn't so. Sounds sort of screwy, doesn't it? But it happens to be the truth.

"And besides, just now it isn't nearly so important to you what *I* think about you, or what your dad or your mother or your teachers or any other old timers like us prehistoric dodoes (yes, I know that's what you think we are) believe about you. Forget it, Bill," (as the older boy started to interrupt) "you don't have to be polite and tactful. I know you fellows think I'll be passing out in a few short years."

"What really rates with all you fellows is what other lads your own age, and even more those who are just a little older than you are, think about how good you are. Harry tries to prove it by beating the other car, or boat. Guys from the wrong side of the railroad track sometimes try to do it by smashing windows, or breaking into a house, or releasing the brakes or slashing the tires of parked cars.

"Hot rods, and motor cyclists—no matter what their age is in years—are just as far from being grown up as ten-year-old kids, when they rely on their souped-up jalopies or their stripped-down motors or their fire-cracker-popping motor cycles to build them up with their own crowd—and with anyone else on the road that they can impress with their show-off antics.

"What determines the particular variety of kid tricks a fellow indulges in isn't so much a matter of his own choice as it is what the rest of his crowd considers he-man stuff. With nine- or ten-year-olders, it may be writing dirty words on the walls of the school toilets. With thirty- or forty-year-old sex offenders, who aren't any more than ten years old emotionally, it may be whispering dirty suggestions to others like themselves, or to innocent kids they can get hold of."

Harry suddenly interrupted, with what was apparently a new idea that had just dawned on him.

"Do you suppose that could be why the Bat Fraternity has those wild hazings and dangerous initiations, the kind that killed that little freshman last year, and nearly broke up the frat? You certainly don't believe that *those* fellows, who every one in school knows are stuck on themselves because they've been tapped by the best and most exclusive club in school—it couldn't be that *they* aren't dead sure of themselves, could it?" and Harry looked as if he just couldn't swallow *that* idea.

"Of course they're not sure of themselves, Harry, any more than you are, or Jack is, or Bill. Just *what* is a snob, and *why* is he, anyway, do you suppose? Or didn't you ever stop to wonder? Well, I'll tell you; and then you try it out on your friends, and see if I'm not right.

"A snob is a person who isn't sure of how he stands with other people, and so low-rates everybody but those he considers his superiors. In this way he tries to make himself feel that he must be better than those who want his approval, and so he hurts them and humiliates them to assure himself of his power over them. When he blackballs a fraternity candidate or turns down an applicant for membership in his 'exclusive' club, he thinks he's showing how much better man he is than the poor helpless boob he's excluding. For every snob has a good bit of the bully in him, you see.

"Another thing younger fellows are nuts about, is the approval of Joes a little older than themselves, though not old enough to be nearing the grave, like their dads or uncles or myself. That's one reason so many fellows pet and even go the limit with girls. It's not for any pleasure or satisfaction they get out of it themselves, but just to show the girls, and other fellows who are the least little bit older, that they are perfectly normal and masculine."

Here Bill, who had been listening with the closest attention, suddenly cut in:

"Do you know, Doc, that's exactly what was eating on me the other night, when I was out with those older guys and got myself into the spot I was so tense about when I came to your office. *I* didn't really want to have anything to do with that skirt. As a matter of fact, she was actually sort of disgusting to me. But I didn't want the others to think there was anything wrong with me, or that I was 'queer,' or that I couldn't rate with the rest of them.

"So I just went ahead and acted like a fool. And all I got out of what I see now was just a fool stunt was several days of sure-enough mental hell, before you told me I hadn't caught any disease but was just imagining things. A dollar will get you five that I won't be *that* sort of a come-on again," and Bill slid back down on the bottom of the boat with a sigh of relief at the mere recollection of his escape from his little private Hades.

"I hate 'dating,'" volunteered Jack, hesitantly. "But it sure does buck me up, to have the other fellows hear girls I've been around with say I've got a cute line, or that I'm no peasant for a tot my size. It really builds me," and Jack, who had been listening in silence up to now, stuck out his chin with a pleased expression of self-satisfaction at what he considered his "sharp" vocabulary, then added:

"But I sure straighten up and die when a deep-pocket wipes me just because he has a big car."

"Deflate, hub cap. Stop acting so sophisticated, and talk plain American," and Harry shoved the subdued Jack over on the thwart with his elbow, then remarked thoughtfully: "I wonder if you can't help me with something else that's bothering me—"

"Maybe so, maybe so, Harry. But first, Jack, get for'ard and cut up some of that bait; and break out the fishing tackle, will you Bill? And for Pete's sake, Harry, give me a crack at that wheel! I brought you loafers along to act as a crew, not for a lot of passengers to keep me from having a little bit of fun myself with my own ship. Get going, sailor," and the doctor pushed Harry to one side, took over the wheel, and gave her the gun. As soon as she reached full speed, he threw the helm over with a flourish, putting her into a tight turn.

Unfortunately for him and his dignity, he had completely failed to notice a very small dinghy at mooring that lay directly in their way as they rounded a point. The skidding speed boat would most certainly have demolished her had it not been for the quick thinking and fast action of Bill and Harry.

Bill grabbed the boat hook and Harry snatched up a paddle, and between them they succeeeded in fending off the dinghy, though she scraped a wide strip of paint off their shiny white side as they shot past her. They all watched her intently as she bobbed crazily up and down in their wake. Then the boys looked at one another in dead silence, but grinning broadly with no attempt to conceal their feelings.

The doctor had the grace to flush guiltily, then looked around sheepishly, to meet the level gaze of Harry, who did his very best to give him the cool, rather scornful look that had gone in the opposite direction earlier in the afternoon, when another collision had been averted. Then he relaxed and chuckled, while the rest of the boys howled with laughter at the doctor's humiliation.

The next minute they had reached the float, and were tumbling helter skelter out of the boat and up the steep bank. The doctor followed them, considerably subdued by his chagrin over the narrow escape he had not deserved after his lubberly trick. They had almost reached the top of the bank when Harry remarked, condescendingly:

"Don't feel too bad about it, Doc. The best of us have to show off sometimes, and come a cropper while doing so," then tripped and fell flat on his face as the doctor's foot shot out and caught him unawares.

"Don't forget the respect due to old age, pal," grinned the doctor; and the account was balanced and closed to the satisfaction of all concerned.

GETTING ALONG WITH DAD

SUPPER WAS OVER. THE FRYING PAN AND TIN PLATES and cups had been hastily scraped and dunked by Jack, the rookie of the crew; and the embers over which they had cooked the fish and boiled the coffee had been replenished with driftwood to make a roaring blaze.

The boys were gathered round it chatting over the day's events. But the talk gradually died down, as the glowing coals took the place of the roaring flames, and cast flickering shadows that lighted the serious faces of the group. Suddenly Bill reached over and poked Harry none too gently in the ribs:

"Wake up, sourball. What's all the gloom about? You look as if you'd swallowed the anchor when we came ashore, instead of dropping it. Tell Papa all your little troubles."

Without deigning to give so much as a glance in Bill's direction, Harry studied the fire a minute or two longer in silence, then turned slowly toward the doctor. "How about doing like you promised you would, and telling me what makes me feel the way I do about my dad? When I was younger I always used to think he was the biggest of the big shots. But now—"

"Well, just how *do* you feel about him now, Harry?" asked the doctor.

"Why, I admire him a lot, more than any other man I know, I guess. He can hire or fire a man, or close a deal, or make a rattling good after-dinner talk with the best of them. Besides, he gives me almost anything I want, though he does make me mad by asking me unnecessary questions about why I want it, and what I do with it after he gives it to me.

"But he gets me all mixed up. And I believe he's just about as confused about me, as I am about myself. One minute he lets me drive one of the cars, even though he knows it's against the law, because I'm not old enough. I'm big for my age, so everyone who sees me driving thinks I'm a lot older. Then the very next day he'll bawl me out because I use my own judgment and buy a tie he doesn't think is so hot, or make a decision about something he thinks I'm too much of a kid to be trusted with making.

"Besides, he nags me and says I'm breaking the law when I drive 65 or a little bit over. Yet he'll push the new Cadillac up to 85 and higher, and then say it's no matter about a fool law because it's perfectly safe on a straightaway—and there's no highway patrolman in sight! I'd just love to see him pinched—no, I guess I wouldn't, really, though it would sure serve him good and right," and Harry shook his head uncertainly and ran his hands through his hair as though he just couldn't make sense of it all.

The doctor sat quietly thinking for a full minute, then began:

"One of the hardest things for a boy to take is for his father to treat him in the confusing way you speak of, Harry. That is, expecting him one minute to act like a mature man, and panning him the next minute for acting as a man would. At the same time, that's the very hardest thing for a father *not* to do!

"But it isn't so strange that a dad finds some difficulty in deciding the tricky question of how far along you are in the scale of development, when you don't know yourself just where you stand. And I can tell you that that's the case with every normal boy, and not with you alone.

"So instead of asking your dad to be patient with you, I'm going to reverse the usual order by putting in a plug for him and asking *you* to try to be patient with *him!* Just do your best, all of you, to be kind to us old birds, and overlook our blunders when we treat you like kids where we ought to treat you like men. And try your best not to expect us to treat you like men and expect more from you than you are grown up enough to put across. Don't blame us too much when we forget for a minute that you are not still the kids you were just a few years ago!"

"But dad can act like a sure-enough pain in the neck at times," argued Jack.

"Admitted. But you youngsters aren't exactly soothing to the neck, yourselves, at times. So try to have a heart, will you?

"As to your dad, Harry, I know and you know that he isn't perfect, and he knows it too, though you'd better not tell him so, if you know what's good for you. No father is, for that matter; I know I wasn't, with my sons. But as far as I'm concerned, I shouldn't want to have a dad that was perfect, and I don't believe you would, either. Yet from what you yourself have just told us, and from what I've seen of him, he must be a pretty good egg. Anyway, I happen to know that he's a heap sight better father than those of a number of boys I know. And that goes for your dad, Bill, and for yours too, Jack.

"So why not take him for what he is, just as we all have to get along with the folks we're brought into contact with in business or social life or school? When he tells you to do what you both know is right, do it, not because it's what he tells you to do, but because it's right, or the law, or what decent folks naturally do.

"When he does something you don't think is quite right, or asks you to do something you don't think he's justified in asking of you, don't argue or fuss at the time, if you don't want to catch a cyclone. Then some time later, be man enough and frank enough to ask his reason for what he did, or asked you to do. Say that you're not criticizing him, but that you are honestly interested in knowing.

"It may be a little hard for him to take, at first; but I know your father pretty well, and I've seen him in some pretty tough spots. I believe that if you'll treat him in this adult way, just as you would treat another man whether of his age of yours, you'll be surprised at the way your relations will improve.

"I know I've had a lot to learn in dealing with my sons. It's hard for us to remember that we were kids too, just as you used to be; but that you and we both have grown up. And you can help us with this tough job of learning to treat you as men and not like the little fellows we used to boss, if you'll remember to try to act like men. We never did own you, even in those days that are gone. We certainly don't own you now."

"Any suggestions as to how I might start?" queried Harry, with the air of someone who was willing to take a chance on anything that seemed reasonable.

"Well, one way would be to make up your mind not to take the opposite side of every question he happens to be discussing at the table or when you happen to have company.

It's a big temptation, I know; but so is monkeying with a buzz saw. I don't mean never to express an honest opinion, nor to agree with everything he says. That would be bootlicking, and that wouldn't help.

"What I mean is to try to see things through the other fellow's eyes, even if the other fellow happens to be your dad. That's good practice for debating. See how it works at home.

"Then, too, it's a good idea to mention something good you may have heard someone say about him. That's not flattery. It's just one of the pleasant things you can do to make life run more smoothly. You'll be surprised at the way he'll take that.

"Still another thing you'd probably never think of doing is mentioning some goodlooking suit of clothes, or snappy tie, or becoming hat, when he first puts them on. You don't have to make up compliments. Just say what you think and feel when it happens to be on the good side. (Take my advice though and keep mum if you think they make him look like something the cat dragged in. That can happen sometimes with us old fellows when we try to dress like one of the boys!) These are all little things, I know. But I know you'll be more than pleased at the way they oil up some of the creaking squeaking spots in the family's daily goings on. One more tip, though. Don't say one of these nice things just before you touch him for a five spot."

The fire was almost out. There was silence. Somehow it didn't seem the time for any more talk. It was time to break camp—and to think some long thoughts. The doctor tossed a bucket of water on the embers, and the boys stamped out the last glowing coals among the ashes. The doctor broke the silence.

"Now pack up the duffel, make everything snug and ship-shape, and let's get going. The last one in the car is a rot—"

"Careful, Doc; no coarse language!" and Jack ducked adroitly as the doctor shied a chunk of firewood at him. Then they filed down the bank in silence, each doing a lot of thinking.

AN AGE-OLD QUESTION

THE DOCTOR HAD INVITED SOME OF THE FELLOWS TO one of his one-night-a-month fireside parties, when they sat around the big log fire and got off their chests some of the things boys talk about and worry over. "One of the doc's get-togethers is better than any high school bull session we ever have," Tom had confided to a friend once. "You can ask that guy *any*thing—nothing you say ever gets him ruffled, he tells you what you want to know, and nobody else ever hears anything about it."

They had been talking over the team's record for the past year, and prospects for the year ahead; and the talk had come round, as it so often does these days, to the question of professionalism in sports, and what is permitted and what is frowned on. After each one had had his say, and the doctor had summed up the sentiment of the group, they fell silent. The lights hadn't been lighted, and only the occasional flare-up of a burning log lit up a thoughtful face here and there round the circle.

At last Bill broke the silence. "It seems to me, doctor, that in all these questions of what's right and what's wrong—athletics, relations with girls, cheating at exams, the honor system, and all the rest of it—it's always the 'don'ts' and never the 'do's' that you moralists keep harping on—"

"Hold it, Bill," the doctor interrupted. "Why do you call me a moralist? And have you ever heard me 'harp' on anything, or rub in what *I* think you ought to do about anything you ask me about?"

"You know he doesn't, Bill," broke in two or three of the group. And Jim continued, "He just gives it to us straight and lets us make up our own minds what we want to do in the spot that we happen to be in, and that we're batting our gums over," and Jim looked around belligerently as if to challege anyone to dispute his defense of their friend.

"Oh yes, I know, I know," retorted Bill a little shortly. "You don't have to defend Doc to me, any of you. But what I mean is, he's always on what folks that are older and supposed to be wiser than we are, think is the right side of the argument, whatever it happens to be. And even though he may not say so in so many words, he always lets us see what he thinks we *ought* to do and hopes we *will* do, without telling us we *have* to do it.

"What I want to know is this. Why is it that the thing a fellow wants to do because it's fun and enjoyable is always the wrong thing that folks disapprove of, while the thing they want us to do, and Doc wants us to do, too, is pretty dull milksop sort of stuff. Don't you see what I mean, sir?" and Bill stopped, as if he knew he hadn't yet made himself clear, though he was sure of his ground.

The others looked uncertain. They didn't want to seem disloyal to their older friend; yet they realized that Bill had touched on something that had puzzled and bothered each one of them when he had had a tough decision to make.

The doctor frowned as he studied the fire—then looked

up relieved, and smiled. "Bill's got something there," he said slowly, as if groping for words with which to express what he was thinking. "Come to think of it, the things I've told you *have* been sort of cold oatmeal, haven't they?

"So often the things folks tell us *not* to do seem so much more fun than what we're told we *ought* to do, that going straight looks like a pretty sad sack sort of a show. The ministers, the Scout leaders, the Sunday School teachers, those of us who really like boys, even the best of us seem to be fighting a losing fight. We always seem to be stopping fellows from doing the things they want to do, and that they feel sure will be good fun, and urging them to do stuff that is as dull as dishwater," and he rubbed his forehead perplexedly.

Suddenly he straightened up in his chair, then leaned forward and gave the fire a vigorous jab with the poker. It sent the sparks flying up the chimney, and started a blaze that lighted up his face as well as those of the rest of the circle. "Men, I believe I've got something!"

The boys looked at him expectantly, then Jim popped out with the word that most of them had been thinking:

"Give!"

"All right, then. You asked for it. Here it is. If you get tired listening, just holler 'Uncle' and I'll quit.

"You all know of course that what Bill has just stumbled on is a bit of philosophizing that is as old as the hills. Folks, whether they're old or young, have always thought that the thing they want to do *right now* is the thing that's the most fun; while the thing that has to be put off till tomorrow or next year isn't worth thinking about, or planning for, or giving up anything for. And that anyone who urges you to wait or save up for the future, is an old fuddy duddy that wants to cheat you out of the good times you're entitled to.

"The old wheeze, 'Let's eat and drink today, for tomorrow we die,' is one way of expressing it. Another is 'Tomorrow's a long way off—this is today.' Still another one is: 'You're only young once—better have a good time while you can.'

"One trouble with that philosophy is that 'today' is over so quickly—and then comes the 'tomorrow' that seemed so far off. So if you've had for only today what tasted or felt or looked good, and have spoiled things for tomorrow when you'll be every bit as anxious for good things as you are today, you've made kind of a fool of yourself. For 'today' is never very long in passing, while there'll be a lot of tomorrows, and tomorrows, and tomorrows that will be pretty dull, if you've used up all your fun today.

"The other trouble is that so often the thing that everyone thinks is going to be so much fun, that it's worth sacrificing tomorrow for it, turns out not to be much fun after all. Somehow you just can't make me believe you think it's always more fun to act like a heel than it is to be a good sport and do the square-shooting thing.

"Do you really mean to tell me that there is any one of you here who would actually have more pleasure doing something that you knew would ruin the whole future of a girl you like, and respect, and have had good times with, than in acting in such a way as to make it possible for those good times to continue? Maybe some day marrying her, if you haven't changed in your feelings toward her in the meantime; or, if you have, seeing her marry some good friend of yours?

"Which would give you more real honest-to-goodness satisfaction—fun, if you prefer to call it that? Acting decent and enjoying every minute of the time you spend with a girl? Or taking her off to some greasy-spoon, juke-box-blaring, hole-in-the-wall beer joint, or sitting for hours in a parked car and doing something you and the girl would both be ashamed of the next day, and the day after that, and every future day you had to live?

"It looks to me as if you'd have to have more 'fun' in one night than I've ever known of anybody's having, to outweigh and overbalance the rotten feelings a decent guy would have all the rest of his born days, for having done a thing like that.

"Some time make the experiment of asking a man with a bad hang-over whether the fun he had getting that way the night before, makes up for the rotten hours of the following day. No, that's not preaching, it's plain common sense.

"How much respect would your dad get from you—and I happen to know from experience that having his son's respect is something a man thinks a lot of—if he wasn't willing to deny himself some fun so as to take out insurance for your mother, or put some money in the bank for your education? I'll venture that the father of every one of you gets more actual satisfaction out of looking at his insurance policy or totting up his bank account, than he'd get out of horsing around in a sporty convertible. And you know as well as I do how touchy they are about the cars they drive, to say nothing of those they would be driving if they weren't thinking more of tomorrow's good times than they are of today's.

"You know these dads of yours aren't pious, or noble. They don't feel self-righteous, either. They're just looking ahead for their satisfaction."

"Oh, come on now, doc," objected Harry disgustedly. "Do you honestly expect us to believe it's more fun to be a goody goody sad sack than to do a little necking after a party?" and he looked round the circle for backing. "Or to spout 'The lips that touch wine shall never touch mine' when a goodlooker offers you a glass of spiked punch at a dance? Or to come home and be able to look your mother in the eye and say, 'Mamma, I've been your good little boy all evening. Aren't you proud of me?' Bah! Phooey!" and Harry spat in the fire to show his disgust at the mere idea.

"Don't ask me, Harry," countered the doctor good-naturedly. "Don't ask the other fellows, either. Just ask yourself. And don't tell me the answer, either. If you can convince yourself it was more fun to eat all that rich stuff when you lost your place on the track team for breaking training before last year's meet, than it would have been to be one of the men who won the interscholastic championship, go right ahead. But I don't believe you can make it stick.

"If you can, then you're a lot different stuff from most of our best ball players and track men. *They* don't call it 'preaching' or 'moralizing' when coach expects them to give up today's fun for tomorrow's 'win' and the celebration that goes along with it. And I don't believe *you* do, either.

"How much did you enjoy your fun the other night, Bill? 'Tomorrow' came mighty soon for you, didn't it? And if you'd contracted the bad luck you thought you had, it would have proved the most expensive fun you'd ever had."

"Heck, it wasn't fun even while I was doing it. I told you that," admitted Bill disgustedly.

"No, and the same way with Harry's 'not being goody goody.' You see—"

"Excuse me for interrupting, doctor," interposed Tom, rather hesitantly. "But what's that purring sound? It sounds to me like—"

"It sounds to me like adenoids, men," shouted Jim from the other end of the circle, with a loud laugh. "Stop that snoring and wake up, little man. It's time for 'itta boys to be tucked in bed. But we'll take good care of you, never fear," and he and Bill dragged poor Jack into the light of the fire. There he stumbled about, rubbing his eyes, while the older boys shouted with laughter and pushed him none too gently hither and yon in the flickering light. The doctor's talk ended abruptly.

"You'll have to excuse us, Doc. But you can see for yourself what a long dull sermon can do to even a highly intelligent congregation," and Jim grinned his widest grin.

"Heraus with you, the whole kit and b'ilin' of you. And don't come around here again inviting me to cast pearls before you swi— you gentlemen," and the doctor got to his feet in mock indignation. "Time to go on home, and see if you can't repent of your lack of respect for my bald gray hairs. Next meeting will be at the lake," and the boys trooped out of the house and down the steps, laughing and talking as they went. The doctor turned back and sat down before the fire, poking it into flames again.

SO LONG, FELLOWS

To The Fellows Who've Stuck It Out and Finished Reading This Book for the First Time

Most books start with a dedication to someone the writer likes and admires and wants to honor. This one goes at things the other way round. For it ends with a dedication.

But it is like other books in one way. It is dedicated to some people the writer likes, and admires, and would like to honor—if he thought they'd let him get away with it and not razz him for doing it.

These people are the Harrys, Jacks, Jims, Toms and Bills he has known, and liked, and admired, and worked with, and had good times with, through the years. A few of them, a very few, are older than he is; a lot more are his own age; while more, far more, of them are a good bit younger.

If you've read this book through, you've learned something about how boys and men are made, and in what ways they are different from girls and women. And you've learned, too, that there is quite a bit to this growing up business that everyone just has to go through.

There's something else, that you may not believe just yet; but you will come to believe it, later on. And that is that to most men, growing up completely means, sooner or later, getting married and having boys, and perhaps girls, of their own. Men and women who don't do this usually seem to feel, as they get on in life, that they've missed some of the very best things life might have given them.

How can you tell that? Well, just look around you at the people you know and respect, the people you hear about over the radio, or see in the current events in the movies or on television, or read about in the papers. Just about every one of them is married, see if they're not. And the time will come when even Jack here, who is so sure of himself now, will tumble, just as most other normal men do.

When that time comes, you are going to be mighty glad you did the right thing, the square thing, the thing you knew was what you ought to do. You're going to be "grown up" a long time. So if you know that what you are doing now is going to contribute to your self-respect and your good health and that of those you love for all those long years ahead, you can get a lot of satisfaction even now in knowing that you are storing up good times instead of bad for yourself in the years to come.

There's something more you've learned about growing up, if you didn't know it before, something that some folks never seem to learn. And that is that growing up isn't something any one can do, like rolling off a log. It takes effort, and plenty of it.

Maybe this book will help you handle some of the difficult things that happen while you're growing up. Maybe it will make it easier for you to understand what it is that makes you feel and think and act the way you do. And maybe it will help you *not* to do some of the things many fellows do hastily, and thoughtlessly, without the slightest idea of the consequences that may not show up until long afterwards—and then regret them for the rest of their lives. For these early mistakes that seem so unimportant have a way of sticking to a fellow the way a burr sticks to a long-haired dog; he just can't seem to shake them off.

And yet, although growing up can be such a difficult, unpleasant, tough job that often throws a fellow completely off balance for a while, it can be a time when he feels pretty good, sometimes so good that it seems as if he could lick the whole world. Maybe this book has helped you feel that way, too.

But every book has got to end sometime, and this one must, too. So it's just

"So long, fellows, I'll be seeing you—I hope!"

INDEX